Take My Ex-Husband, Please  But Not Too Far

BARBARA MALLEY

Little, Brown and Company

Boston   Toronto   London

FIRST EDITION

The names of several characters herein portrayed have been changed
to protect their privacy.

Cartoons and painting by Darrell McClure.

LIBRARY OF CONGRESS CATALOGING-IN-PUBLICATION DATA

Malley, Barbara.
    Take my ex-husband, please—but not too far / by Barbara
Malley.—1st ed.
        p.   cm.
    ISBN 0-316-54524-4
    1. Divorced women—United States—Case studies.   2. Malley,
Barbara.   3. Malley, Edward.   I. Title.
HQ834.M25   1991
306.89′082—dc20   90-46578

                10 9 8 7 6 5 4 3 2 1
                             BP

Designed by Barbara Werden
Published simultaneously in Canada by Little, Brown & Company
(Canada) Limited

Dedicated, with love and admiration,
to Kathie White, my comfort,
my joy, my daughter

"Humor is emotional chaos remembered
in tranquility."

JAMES THURBER

Contents

Acknowledgments

My gratitude to Little, Brown's Colleen Mohyde, part editor, part sculptor. She knew precisely what to subtract from a massive manuscript and how to chisel the remainder into its present form.

I am grateful, too, for the generous input of my daughter Kathleen White; my sons, Ted and Tim Malley; my sister, Janeth Black; and my friend Edward Malley.

Three other friends offered bountiful support: reliable consultant Richard White, and faithful allies Maureen Malley and Kathy Malley. Thank you, darlings, for marrying my children.

A warm hug for Ellee Avakian, whose Oriental brush class led me to a new kind of creativity as well as to several supportive new friends.

I am not likely to forget a phone call from Little, Brown's vice president and publisher, Roger Donald. "I love your book," he said. What sweeter words could fall on a would-be author's ears?

My starry-eyed thanks to agent Don Congdon, who thought enough of my book to add me to his Who's Who roster of clients. Who, me? Will wonders never cease.

Introduction

The fine predicaments in this book span half a century and include love, courtship, unexpected pregnancies, divorce, living in sin, boat sinkings, and plane crashes. In other words, if you live long enough, almost anything can happen. And if you have a penchant for jotting it all down, from the sublime to the ridiculous to the scary, the next thing you know, you've written a book.

My son Tim was the first to point this out. After reading several decades' worth of my diaries and letters, he announced, "Hey, Mom, someday when you're gone I'm going to put your stuff in a book and make a fortune."

"Now hold on just a darn minute," I said. If Tim's hunch wasn't a pipe dream, my heavenly reward could jolly well wait.

Rereading the "stuff" with new eyes, Tim's eyes, it began to assume a different aspect. It was clear that individual letters would interest only my children and grandchildren, but the fifty-year relationship between the father of my children and me—a story both old-fashioned, yet thoroughly modern—might find a wider audience.

The groundwork for this book started in 1960 when I read an article in *Reader's Digest,* "What Writing Letters Can Do for You." The author, Flora Rheta Schrieber, said, "Capturing and holding the precious experiences of the past, letters are the emissaries of our former to our present selves. . . . Many persons make letters into an improvised diary. Pasting those they receive and carbons of those they write into a scrapbook, they find the result far more revealing than a formal diary."

I had often wondered how, if anything happened to me, anyone could make head or tail of the scribbles I had amassed over the years. Schrieber's article gave me the impetus I needed to type up my huge hoard of letters and diaries. When my collection was complete, it would be like having a photograph album to muse over, except the family would be portrayed in words instead of pictures.

Why did I report minor and major events in my life in such copious detail? Partly to entertain my correspondents and partly to keep my diaries up-to-date. Since my memory is a sieve, articles published in boating and flying magazines owed their existence to my habit of recording experiences as they happened. Without these records I would doubtless recall a plane crash, but its details would soon have faded.

As my writing technique developed, I learned that *mis*adventures provided the most satisfactory material. The more things turned sour, the more I felt challenged to make lemonade from lemons. I won't say I rejoiced in calamities, but they did come with a saving grace. After I'd rallied from the latest shock, I'd reach for my therapeutic pencil and let it go to work. Invariably my distress would dissipate and a bad day would end on an upbeat note. As my mother wrote to my sister, Janeth, "Barbara is discovering what fun it is to ride a pencil like a witch on a broomstick."

I was seventeen in 1938 when I met Eddie Malley at a surprise birthday party for Betty Allen. I was sitting on a Ping-Pong table, swinging my legs, when an attractive young man asked me if I wanted to play. Thus began a turbulent courtship that eventually became what was known as a scandal in that innocent, bygone era. Mother had never warned me about where a game of Ping-Pong could lead.

My penniless but confident young suitor often assured my skeptical mother that someday he would be a big success. "Maybe I'll even be taking care of *you*," he predicted jauntily.

Sooner than he expected, Ed found himself converting his father's trucking garage, first to the North Terminal Rental Company, then to a small manufacturing plant contributing to the war effort. When peace was declared, North Terminal Machine Company was probably the smallest plant in the country to earn an Army-Navy E with two stars, denoting continued high achievement in war production. Ed considered entering the service but was turned down; he was told his work at North Terminal was essential.

After the war Ed continued to build up the truck rental business he had started without much more than bravado and the ability to sell himself. By the time our fourth child arrived, shortly after my twenty-fifth birthday, we had moved into a rambling old house in Cohasset. For the next two decades my mother lived with us happily in her third-floor quarters overlooking the ocean. She spent her winters in the Fort Lauderdale house Ed bought in 1950 as an investment and a vacation haven. No one was prouder of my husband's achievements than my mother; she rejoiced in the warmth and laughter and affection that pervaded our household.

Raising the children over the next twenty years meant hectic times, but, aside from inevitable problems with our teenagers, Ed and I were able to look back on many happy experiences. In 1953, he fulfilled his lifelong dream of buying a boat, which provided fun and relaxation for the family. We enjoyed fishing trips with the children, but we also enjoyed getting away alone to Provincetown or Martha's Vineyard.

During the summer of 1961 our older son, Ted, got a job handling freight at Logan Airport. Someone took him for an airplane ride, and the next thing we knew, we had a pilot in the family. Ed was darned if he'd let the kid get ahead of him, and I couldn't let either of them get ahead of me. Thus began one of the most satisfying experiences Ed and I had ever shared. In 1964 he was appointed to the Massachusetts Aeronautics Commission, serving for eight years. As for me, between boating, flying, and raising a family, there was never a dearth of material for my letters and diaries.

Early in 1988 I renewed a correspondence with a friend, Edward Brecher, and told him I was trying to write a book but had bogged down. An experienced editor, Brecher began reviewing my manuscript. When he questioned me about my early relationship with Ed, I swamped him with another deluge. I felt like a literary sorcerer's apprentice.

The sorcerer, unfazed, found an island in my flood of recollections. "For almost fifty years," he wrote, "you and Ed have shared a remarkable, enduring, and unusual relationship—courtship, marriage, divorce, and courtship again, sometimes with each other, sometimes not. This should be the focus of your book."

With Ed Brecher's encouragement and guidance, I lifted a love story from my rambling memoir. It starts with a letter I wrote to a stranger named Darrell McClure . . .

One

Ed Boatguy
(1954–1956)

October 21, 1954
Cohasset, Massachusetts
To Darrell McClure

Dear Mr. McClure:

   I am writing to ask a favor. My husband, Ed, has been sub-scribing to *Yachting* magazine for many years and is an ad-mirer of your cartoons. When I was recently trying to think of a Christmas gift for the man who has everything nautical, it occurred to me that you might consider drawing a person-alized sketch for him. Certainly nothing would please him more. I realize the enclosed check isn't much for a man of your reputation, but it's all my bank account can spare.

   If you accept, the following may help you find an appropri-ate theme:

   What Captain Malley *really* needs for Christmas is a gift certificate to a psychiatrist's office. He is a rabid perfectionist

Captain Ed and First Mate, 1953.

about everything pertaining to our boat, the *Happy Days*,* but when it comes to extracting a few dollars for household repairs, I might as well ask him for one of his eyes.

Consider the matter of the bathroom linoleum, stained and faded and so cracked the rugs had humps in them.

"New linoleum," sobbed my husband. "Why, I bought you new linoleum ten years ago!"

A few days later, however, Ed breezed into the house with a box full of linoleum samples and said cheerfully, "Pick a color."

"Is this a game?" I asked.

---

* The *Happy Days* is a forty-foot twin-screw Matthews power boat that some people might call a yacht or cabin cruiser. Ever since Captain Malley installed outriggers, he prefers to call it a Sport Fisherman.

"No," he said, looking hurt. "We need new linoleum. You know better than I about things like colors."

Hastily, before he could change his mind, I chose a practical bathroom design.

Ed was shocked. "That one! On a *boat?*"

There followed a brisk exchange of opinions. Don't misunderstand me, Mr. McClure; my husband and I have no differences that couldn't be settled by the Supreme Court. This time we compromised: new linoleum was installed throughout the *Happy Days;* she was freshly painted inside and out; new curtains and slipcovers were ordered for her. Meanwhile, back at the ranch, the bathroom is now resplendent in black marbleized linoleum.

According to Ed, most of his extravagances (he calls them "investments") have been in the interest of safety. Inclined to be safety-conscious since our first boat, the *Barbara,* sank under us, he is determined to be prepared for any contingency except bankruptcy. Since we have been unable to find anyone with enough derring-do to buy what's left of the *Barbara,* we are the only folks in town who own, not one, but *two* boats we can't afford. Without blinking an eyelash, Ed will dash off checks for such things as a ship-to-shore telephone, built-in CO_2 system, or automatic pilot. But mention a new lampshade or shoes for the kiddies and he clutches his heart, or his wallet.

In spite of all this, however, there isn't a boat in the world I'd rather have. I'd even settle for the same captain.

October 28, 1954
Old Saybrook, Connecticut

From Darrell

Yes, lady, I'll draw up a sketch for you and Ed Boatguy and tear up your check. Your letter is sufficient payment. I'm sending your letter to the brains at *Yachting* to see if it can be used as material in some fashion.

November 12, 1954
Cohasset

To Darrell

I am, of course, delighted that you will do a Darrell Mc-Clure cartoon for Ed. And gratis, yet!

I have been remembering other adventures that might be grist for your mill. One evening last summer, Ed and I dropped the hook in Provincetown Harbor and, breaking out our new outboard motor, putted ashore to have dinner. We visited all the bars and explored all the shops, and I only regretted we couldn't eat in all the restaurants. Toward midnight we made our way back to the beach where the dinghy was pulled up. The sand bit my legs and angry waves slapped at the shore. We had failed to notice a brisk wind developing.

Removing our shoes, Ed and I dragged the dinghy into the water, hopped in, and started the outboard. We had gone only a few yards when a wave drenched us—and the outboard motor. Wading back to shore, we tipped the water out of the dinghy and set off again, this time with a pair of oars.

"Now don't you wish we'd built that terrace instead?" I asked, congratulating myself that I hadn't lost my sense of humor. I could tell that Ed had lost his by the look he gave me.

The shadowy outline of the *Happy Days,* pitching and tossing, loomed ahead. Ed brought us close enough to the stern for me to grab the ladder. Then the dinghy heaved and I lost my grip. At the same time Ed lost one of the oars. Half-swamped, the dinghy was rapidly being swept from the boat when Ed grabbed the dinghy painter and plunged overboard.

I had married Ed, despite qualms, when I was an eighteen-year-old, slightly pregnant Smith College freshman wishing I didn't have to. Now, as he fought through the waves to the Matthews with me in tow, I realized once again, with awe, that I had unwittingly married the right man.

"Go below and change into dry clothes," Ed ordered in his Captain Bligh voice when we were safely on board. I meekly went below. "Come up here and hold the flashlight while I bail out the dinghy," he called a minute later.

I started to say "Wait till I get some clothes on," then thought better of it. This was no time for niceties. Ed bailed out the dinghy while I stood by with the flashlight, wearing only a look of admiration.

The next day we were almost back to Cohasset when our engine conked out off Scituate. Ed worked over it until the sun went down and it grew cold. He always considers it a personal affront when anything goes wrong with his boat, and rescue by the Coast Guard is a fate worse than drowning—but this was a crisis. Reluctantly, Ed sent up flares.

While the Coast Guard was towing us in, Ed gave me my orders. "The minute we touch the dock, you run into town and find a taxi. I'll brush these fellows off as quickly as possible. They'll want to make a big thing of it and have our pictures in the paper—"

"Oh, boy, pictures!" I said, whipping out my mirror and comb.

"—but there won't be any publicity if I can help it," Ed concluded firmly.

When we reached the dock I scrambled up the ladder, bundled to the ears in Ed's big windbreaker, and slipped off in search of a taxi. The Coast Guard, noting my disguise and disappearance, and Ed's evasiveness when they questioned him, put two and two together.

"Oh, we understand perfectly, sir," one said with a leer. "Yes, sir, we'll see that there's no publicity." They clapped Ed Boatguy on the back and winked and would no doubt have pinned a medal on his chest if they'd had one handy. For the next two weeks Ed swaggered.

With warm regards from Ed, the four kids, and the Other Woman, as I now call myself.

November 26, 1954
Fort Lauderdale, Florida

From Darrell

I don't know if you've ever done any professional writing, but believe me, you should. With only one husband, two boats, four children and undoubtedly dogs and/or cats to raise, you could easily find the time.

The sketch that I have drawn would make a good job for *Yachting*, assuming that I have your permission. S'posin' we let *Yachting* run it. Captain Edward Malley, Jr., would see it in print for the first time. Then *whammo*, you could present the original drawing to him. Would you like that?

December 10, 1954
Cohasset

To Darrell

What a dear man you are to dream up the *whammo* idea for Ed. I'm trying to convince him it's only the Christmas season that is making me twinkle all over; but he's beginning to wonder if I have another man in my life. Aha! I do.

Are you ready for another Captain Malley yarn?

Last summer we took a man from Detroit on a fishing trip. But this wasn't just any stray man. Hubert Kent was a purchasing agent for the Ford Motor Company, whom Ed had met on a business trip a few weeks earlier. Mr. Kent mentioned that he would be vacationing on the Cape in August.

"Look me up," Ed said, "and I'll take you out fishing."

Rather to his surprise, the man took him at his word. Ed came home beaming one night and told me we were taking Mr. Kent on a shark-fishing trip.

"Is this likely to get you a Ford contract?" I asked.

"*Shh,*" hissed Ed, turning pale and looking over his shoulder. "Don't *ever* say things like that! If this guy thought I was taking him fishing just because he's a Ford purchasing agent, it would queer things for sure!"

Hubert Kent thoroughly enjoyed his day aboard the *Happy Days*. A whale sounded not far from the boat and had its picture taken for the folks back home in Detroit. We spotted several sharks; a big one hooked himself long enough to convince Mr. Kent that shark fishing was the greatest sport in the world.

"Mummy, look what I found on the beach!" our daughter Vonnie called, thrusting something black and wet in my face, when we returned home with our guest. It looked and smelled like a dead dog.

"How can I dry him out, do you think he'll dry out if I put him in the sun? Doesn't he look *real?*"

Our son Timmy was simultaneously jabbering that his new kite was caught in a big tree. Should he call the fire department to get it down?

"Um-hum," I said, meaning yes, the dead dog did look real; but Timmy went off to call the fire department. I told my older daughter, Kathie, to take our guest upstairs and show him where to change while I set out the caviar and pâté de foie gras. Mr. Kent had barely left the room when Timmy piped up, "Is Daddy going to get the contract?"

"*Shh!* Timmy, will you shut up, for God's sake!" I whispered, aghast.

"Well, all I want to know is, did he—"

I clapped my hand over his mouth. "Where did he ever get an idea like that?" I asked Kathryn, our housekeeper.

"Urmph, rrurmph," said Timmy, squirming.

"I don't know, Mrs. Malley," Kathryn said. "He's been talking like that all day. You know how he is when he gets an idea in his head. I thought maybe he heard you and Mr. Malley talking."

Timmy was still wriggling.

"Timmy, I'm going to let you go, but if you *dare* say *one more word* like that—well, I don't know what your father will do to you."

"What's Timmy done now?" asked Ed, appearing on cue.

I told him. Ed glanced wildly upstairs, then started for Timmy. "I'll strangle him, I swear I'll strangle him!"

"Why can't I just ask—," Timmy began calmly, not at all intimidated.

"Timmy," I pleaded, while his father collapsed in a chair, "not now. Tomorrow. Do you understand? Tomorrow you can ask all the questions you want."

"Who the devil told him, anyway?" Ed asked.

"Nobody told me. I saw the license plate and I knew you went to Detroit to get some business and I read in a funnybook about a guy taking another guy on his boat because he was trying to get a contract."

"I give up," Ed said weakly. "I'm never going to work again. I'll just retire and let this genius support us."

February 15, 1955
Cohasset

To Darrell

Thank you for writing so enthusiastically to *Yachting*'s editor about my yarns. I've written Mr. Rimington suggesting as an article possibility the time our first boat sank. I didn't tell him my contribution in that hour of peril was to keep running to the head. When the water in the cabin was waist-deep, the trip to the head was pointless—and, according to Ed, downright dangerous. He ordered me to go above and *stay* above.

What finally happened to this courageous couple? Did they

go down with their vessel, never to be heard from again? Learn the spine-tingling details in the next issue of *Yachting!*

Perhaps I should write instead about the time we were trying to tie up to a pier in Provincetown. I was at the topside controls and Ed was forward with a line that he intended to toss over one of the pilings rising above our heads.

"You're going too fast," he called. "Put her in neutral."

I obeyed, but our momentum was carrying us past the piling.

"Reverse, reverse!" he shouted.

I shoved the *Barbara* into reverse. The throttle was still pushed up, so we shot backward. The result was curious. Ed had neglected to secure the other end of his line to a cleat. As the boat leapt from under him, he made a wild grab for the line, and before I could say "What on earth are you doing, dear?" he was hanging from the Provincetown pier. I eventually retrieved him, getting paid for my trouble with a dour "What's so funny?"

Another time Ed was climbing down from our cruiser into another when his foot slipped and he fell between the two boats. To this day he wonders what made him so clumsy. It was spilled mayonnaise. Rather than upset him, I let him keep on wondering.

Twice Ed has fallen overboard while trying to harpoon a shark. He insists, from his armchair in front of the TV set, that the sharks we harpoon are just big old harmless sand sharks—but I never saw a pair of arms and legs move as fast as Ed's did when he saw a harmless old shark fin coming toward him. It was like one of those animated cartoons where someone dives into the water, the projector is reversed, and whoosh—he's back on the diving board.

Then there was the breezy Saturday I went for a sail with our friends the Remicks on their sloop, the *Marionette*. Ed was at his office all morning, but early that afternoon he fol-

"I shoved the 'Barbara' in reverse. She shot back like a squid in a hurry. The result was interesting"

lowed us out in the Matthews. Approaching a sailboat safely with a motor cruiser is not a simple maneuver. Ed made several vain attempts to throw Ray a line.

This was a challenge, so Ed devised a new strategy. He cut the motor and climbed into the dinghy, holding the line attached to the *Happy Days*. The plan was for Ray to keep making passes at the skiff until Ed succeeded in throwing him the line.

The first few passes failed. "Let's try once more, Ed!" Ray shouted. A captain for Northeast Airlines, he wasn't the type to give up easily.

This time Ray caught the line. As it curved out in a great arc between the *Happy Days* and the *Marionette*, I cheered. Ray quickly secured his end of the line and as it grew taut, guess who was caught in the middle?

A few feet above the water, the line whipped across the skiff like a knife. To avoid being decapitated, Captain Malley grabbed it with both hands and BOING!—he flipped through the air like a stone from a slingshot.

We now had the Matthews in tow, as planned, but her

"The line whipped across the skiff like a knife.
To avoid being decapitated, my husband grabbed
it with both hands and BOING!"

skipper was rapidly receding in the distance. I was wringing my hands and babbling that I wanted my husband back.

"Calm down!" barked Ray, another one of those guys who think they're Captain Bligh just because they own a boat.

We came about and plowed toward Ed, who was sitting soddenly in the skiff. Ray released the *Happy Days* and Ed climbed aboard, shouting that he had had it, he was going ashore.

"Don't let him go without me," I wailed.

"Oh, my Lord!" groaned Ray.

It was decided that Ed would bring our cruiser alongside the *Marionette*. If he could get near enough without damaging the boats, I was to transfer from one to the other—about as easy as transferring from one galloping horse to another, but the only one worried about possible damage to me was I.

Ed eased the *Happy Days* toward the *Marionette* until the two boats were plunging along neck and neck, with Ray's wife, Dottie, at the tiller of the *Marionette*. Ray was standing by me at the rail to help me across and I was saying uneasily, "Hey, can't you slow this thing down?"

Busy concentrating on the necessary split-second leap, Ray ignored my question, yelled, "Okay, *now!*"—and gave me a push.

I grabbed for the *Happy Days* with one hand and gripped Ray firmly with the other. Result: Ray and I both wound up on the Matthews. This failed to improve Ray's disposition.

Ed and Dottie soon had the two boats plowing along side by side again, and Ray transferred back. He didn't wave.

I've often wondered how Dottie copes with the strain of being married to a pilot. Boating provides more than enough excitement for the Malleys, thank you.

Darrell, the whole family has enjoyed *The Best of Darrell McClure* tremendously. Would you be kind enough to autograph the enclosed copy for me?

February 24, 1955
Fort Lauderdale
From Darrell

Your letter has floored me completely!!! I howled and pounded the floor. I have forwarded both your letters to Ham de Fontaine at *Yachting*.

March 1, 1955
Cohasset
To Darrell

Would *Yachting* be interested in my Protestant-ethic up-bringing versus Ed's prodigality? My father was a "waste not, want not" man who successfully imprinted his views on his children. I grew up knowing the value of a dime as well as a dollar; my bankbook was my favorite reading. But Dad had no way of foreseeing I would marry a man who thinks a bank is something you find by the edge of a river.

Take our Matthews. When we acquired her in the fall of 1953, she was probably the most completely equipped Sport Fisherman on the Eastern Seaboard. Since then, Ed has added so much paraphernalia I often wonder what keeps her afloat.

Semper paratus, the *Happy Days* now has a ship-to-shore telephone, gasoline sniffer, recording fathometer, auxiliary gasoline generator, extra 134-gallon fuel tank, automatic pilot, electric winch, automatic bilge pump, and two new 185-horsepower Gray engines.

Also in the "Be Prepared" category is our collection of charts. Captain Ed is chart-happy. Besides owning a complete set for our local waters around Massachusetts Bay and the Cape, he can often be found poring over charts of Florida and the Bahamas. Who knows, we might take a cruise down the Inland Waterway someday. We might want to explore Flor-

The man is chart happy

ida's swamps and canals, or cross from one coast to another via Lake Okeechobee. We'd be pretty foolhardy to try that without charts.

An elaborate radio direction finder was installed at what I divined was considerable expense. (No one ever gives me a financial report; I just divine these things.) Then along came loran, and what self-respecting Sport Fisherman owner could be satisfied with a mere radio direction finder when a more expensive substitute was available? Ed was only slightly taken aback when he found that the loran requires a 32-volt system. Our 12-volt system had never been adequate anyway, he decided. While he was at it, he might as well add a 110-volt inverter.

"From now on," he promised, "you'll even be able to run a small vacuum cleaner."

"O joy," I said.

Besides wanting to stay afloat, Ed likes to catch fish. When I used to go fishing with my father, the procedure was simple. You put some weights on a line and a clam on the hook and you let the line down until you felt a thud. Next you pulled it up a couple of feet and jiggled. Then you hauled in a nice fat cod.

My husband's fishing is different. First of all, he insists that anything under ten pounds is not a fish. It's bait. Handlines he considers quaint souvenirs of a bygone age. To catch a "real" fish it is necessary to invest in: a built-in fish box, including a circulating live-fish well; every available size and style of fishing rod, reel, and lure; harpoons and barrels; a bow rail to pen in overexuberant harpoon throwers. (Ed has a way of following the harpoon.) Next we had to have a lookout platform, as standing on tiptoe with the binoculars was getting us nowhere. Nothing would do, of course, but the best: an A-frame designed by Eldredge-McGinnis, constructed of hollow spars, complete with a steadying sail.

Ever since we moved to Sandy Cove in Cohasset, I have yearned for a front lawn like normal people's. My husband claims he honestly prefers our yard in its beautiful wild state; I claim he honestly prefers not mowing lawns.

Last spring he surrendered. (This was about the time he ordered the more powerful ship-to-shore phone.) I employed a landscape architect who decided after only an hour of meditation that we had too many trees.

"Oh, dear," I said.

Ed has a passion for trees. He even loves *dead* trees. He's had a complex about trees ever since we lost so many in the hurricane.

All day I plotted my strategy. Ed thinks I wind him around my little finger, but I had a feeling that this time it would take six dray horses and a winch.

"Say, honey," I said, after mellowing him with a T-bone and stacking the dishwasher single-handed. "You know that jungle you call a yard? Well, today I think I saw a bear in it."

"We are not cutting down any trees," my husband said distinctly through his newspaper, rattling it for emphasis.

"Oh," I said.

Maybe you think this discouraged me, Darrell. Not at all. I just bided my time, and on approximately the same day that I saw eye to eye with him on the two new 185-horsepower Gray engines, he saw eye to eye with me on weeding out all those scrubby little trees.

The landscape architect tied strips of cotton around the ancient elms she wanted spared. Shortly afterward the contractors marched in and weeded out the elms.

Miss Griffin said later she had clearly told the contractors to leave standing all trees marked with cotton strips. The contractors said they had clearly told Miss Griffin to mark the trees she wanted eliminated. What my husband said clearly shocked even me.

That was *some* autograph you sent; and the following members of the family wish to thank you: Captain Edward, his first mate, and the four young pirates—plus the "furred and feathered Malleys," namely, our cocker spaniel, Minxi, our black cat, Dizzy, and seven parakeets whose names escape me. Of us all, I think Minxi was the most appreciative; I *know* she's never received an autograph.

We're going to Nassau for the two older kids' spring vacation. If you're still in Fort Lauderdale, maybe we could stop by and say hello before we return to Massachusetts.

March 5, 1955
Fort Lauderdale

From Darrell

I am beginning to feel sorry for Ed Boatguy. Judging by the picture you sent me, I would say he is a man of quiet dignity and rightfully proud of his achievements both afloat and ashore. What happens to him shouldn't happen to a dog. We all make boo-boos from time to time which we hope to bury sight unseen in the dark of the moon, but what chance does *this* poor character have with a female Samuel Pepys trailing his every footstep with notebook in hand and a glint in her eye?

I still want to hear about The Sinking of the *Barbara*. And do let me know exactly when you may be down here.

March 13, 1955
Cohasset

To Darrell

Correction, please. The only time my husband could be described as a man of quiet dignity is when he's asleep. He's different, he's refreshing, he's a wag—but dignified, no. Everyone in town is charmed by him, from the most affluent mechanic to the lowliest banker. They say, "Barbara, you're a good kid and we like you, but that husband of yours—what a character!"

At parties, where is the most laughter, the most entertaining conversation? Wherever Ed Malley is. Usually I am too far away to participate in the hilarity because social custom decrees that a wife with a husband like Ed should be maneuvered as far from him as possible. Someday I'm going to put on a disguise and see if I can worm my way into the inner circle. I could go as a worm. Or as Samantha Pepys, notebook at the ready.

You asked about The Sinking. Our first boat was a thirty-two-foot cabin cruiser built in Ed Boatguy's manufacturing plant by several of his craftsmen in their spare time and a half. From the day of her maiden voyage on wheels down Commercial Street to Boston Harbor until the day she sank, life aboard the *Barbara* was full of surprises.

On the afternoon she was due to be delivered to Sandy Cove, Captain Ed paced the beach in front of our house, binoculars in one hand, movie camera in the other. I lay prone on the sand, brooding over *House Beautiful*. In my opinion we needed a terrace, a driveway, and new shoes far more than we needed a boat.

When the *Barbara* cruised into the cove, our neighbors gathered to look her over and pull her apart. One of them didn't like her color. (I had suggested light blue but Ed thought I said *bright* blue.) Another thought she was poorly proportioned.

"Kind of top-heavy," said a third. Suddenly I found myself bristling with loyalty.

"So is Marilyn Monroe," I retorted.

The boat did look top-heavy, because the roof of the cabin was seven feet high—another of my suggestions. I wanted room for windows instead of portholes, so Barbara Galley Slave could see where we were going.

Our stateroom was on the small side, but comfortable if we curled up like snails. By way of compensation the cockpit was big enough for four or five couples and several large tuna.

We have never caught a tuna. We have never *seen* a tuna, but we have reduced the shark population considerably. Sharks can be caught on rod and reel or speared with a harpoon attached to plenty of line wrapped around a barrel. As a rule we prefer the thrill of harpooning them. That is, Ed prefers the thrill of harpooning them. I prefer taking pictures.

It was lovely mid-September weather, but a bit choppy, the day the *Barbara* began taking in water a mile and a half north of Boston Lightship. My friend Marion Marsh and I were chatting over our beer and sandwiches when we noticed that Wes Marsh was diligently operating the hand pump while Ed was rushing around examining sea cocks, toilet fittings, and sink drains.

"Must be a leak somewhere," said Marion.

"How about another beer?" I said.

I went below for the beer and found myself in water up to my ankles. "Hey, Ed," I called. "There's a lot of *water* down here!"

"I know it," Ed called back. "We're sinking. If we had the tender, I'd row to the Lightship for help."

Marion and I went topside and vainly jumped up and down, waving our jackets and shouting at the Lightship. Ed handed us horns and flares. We set off the flares and blew on the horns until we were purple. Ed and Wes tied several kapok pillows together and took off all the hatches, lashing them into a makeshift raft. Then we huddled together on the flying bridge, awaiting our fate.

We sighted a sail leisurely dipping along the horizon, then coming about and heading directly toward us. The nearer it drew, the stiffer became our upper lips. Soon we were cracking jokes and being very British about the whole thing. Our rescuer, it turned out, was George Crocker in the *Tango*.

"Nice to see you, George," Ed called—the greatest understatement since Henry M. Stanley's "Dr. Livingstone, I presume?"

Marion, Wes, and I swam to the *Tango*, and George helped us aboard. Ed remained on the *Barbara*, sadly surveying the scene. For a moment I had the impression he had decided to go down with his ship. He chose instead to help the harbormaster tow our partially submerged boat to the beach near the yacht club.

With the assistance of his insurance company, the *Barbara* was eventually restored to her former almost seaworthy condition.

When we acquired our Matthews the following season, a group of friends assembled to help christen her. The *Happy Days* was absolutely boo-boo-proof, Ed assured me.

Then someone got locked in the head and someone fell overboard while attempting to give upside-down advice through the porthole. I'm not mentioning any names.

March 25, 1955
Cohasset

To Darrell

I've written you about Ed's tendency to fall overboard, but there was one occasion when he didn't *fall*.

We had cruised down to Osterville with our neighbors the Thaxters to visit a bachelor friend, Keith, in a cottage on the harbor. There had been a party ashore Saturday night, and as the scene opens, Jayne and I have returned to the Matthews. We are waiting for our husbands to rejoin us. It is already 2:00 A.M.

"I wonder what's keeping them," Jayne said.

At 2:15 A.M. I dug out the searchlight and beamed it at Keith's living room window. The porch light winked coyly a few times in reply, but there was no other sign of action.

At 2:30 I had an inspiration. "We don't have to sit here like dummies. Why don't we go in and fetch them?"

"Do you know how to run the outboard?"

"Well, no—but I can row."

"No thank you," Jayne said. "I'll stand here and guide you in with the searchlight."

I cast off, and after going around in circles a few times (guided by Jayne with the searchlight), I began to get the hang of it. It was really chunky out, and there was something the matter with one oarlock. The oar kept slipping out, and by the time I'd get it righted Jayne would holler that I was heading out to sea.

As I neared the dock, I was not cheered by the sound of raucous laughter—mostly my husband's—floating out over

"I stood there dripping on the Welcome mat"

the water. I pictured that vivacious Stella from New York sitting on his lap and running her fingers through his hair. She was kind of attractive; in fact, the more I brooded about her, the more she looked like Doris Day.

Pulling up to the pier, with one foot on the ladder and the other in the stern, I fell in. I managed to keep my hair dry and sloshed up the ladder—wringing wet from the neck down. Someone must have tipped off the revelers that the enemy was storming the ramparts.

"Coming, dear. We were just leaving. We'll be right there," Ed sang out. I stood there dripping on the welcome mat. Someone laughed.

"It's no laughing matter," I fumed as we walked back to the dock. "The dinghy capsized. I might have drowned."

Ed stopped short. "You capsized the *dinghy?* Oh, my outboard motor," he moaned. "It'll be ruined!"

That's when I pushed him in.

April 4, 1955
Fort Lauderdale
From Darrell

I'll bet you haven't done a single thing about that article for *Yachting*. You should. How can your hardworking husband seek honest retirement if you don't start bringing some money into the house? Think of your hungry children. In other words, shake the lead out!

August 6, 1955
Old Saybrook
From Darrell

So you dunnit, you doll you! Sold your story to *Yotting!* I'm proud of you. Now they say I'll have to illustrate the thing. How do I get mixed up in these affairs, anyway?

Barbara meets pen pal Darrell McClure
in Fort Lauderdale, 1969.

January 16, 1956
Cohasset

To Darrell

Your illustrations are priceless, Darrell. The article is creating a flurry here in Cohasset. A number of friends have conveyed their condolences to "poor Ed" and asked me questions like: "Is he speaking to you yet?" or "When is the divorce?"

Can I help it if he keeps supplying me with material?

Two

For Better, for Worse, or Whatever
(1956–1962)

When we weren't having adventures on the high seas, we resided in a rambling old house in Cohasset bursting with people and pets. In addition to our four spirited children, there was my mother, always busy writing poetry and stories for children; my childhood caretaker, Vaughan, whom I'd promised a "place by the chimney corner" in her old age; and our housekeeper, Kathryn, who somehow managed to adjust to the stresses and strains of our lively ménage and menagerie. We all lived together in a sort of frantic harmony—four children, four women, and, last but not least, that most patient and generous of men, Ed. Occasionally my husband and I escaped to the relative peace of our Fort Lauderdale vacation home.

Ed and Barbara and the Malley brood.
Left to right: *Kathie, Teddy, Timmy, and Vonnie, 1948.*

February 12, 1956
Fort Lauderdale, Florida

We are enjoying our vacation with Ed's dad and step-mother—although Tina and I occasionally have Trouble in the Kitchen. She doesn't read instructions, she does things backwards, but her meals are out of this world. One night I insisted on getting dinner by myself—I wanted to try the Seven-Heat Economy Cooker that came with our stove—and burned the potatoes. Tina and Eddie kept assuring me they were tastier that way ("just like campfire potatoes," said Tina), but Grandpa, unaware that I had taken over the cooking, wanted to know what the hell had happened to the potatoes.

Tina keeps putting the table butter in the refrigerator. I keep switching it to the cupboard because I dislike mutilating my toast when I spread it. Yesterday morning I left the butter dish on the hot stove and it ranneth over. I also cremated the toast, which wouldn't have happened if Tina hadn't confused me by changing the toaster's dial. Fortunately, the folks weren't up yet. It took me half an hour to eliminate all traces of disaster, but it was worth it. Never let it be said that Ed is dieting in self-defense.

Ed and his dad don't always see eye to eye on things, either. In fact, if one discovers he's agreeing with the other, he switches sides. The trouble is, they're both bossy. Or to put it another way, they're both leaders. (That's the way Ed puts it.) Grandpa has a habit of treating Ed as if he were still his little boy instead of a grown man who has a license and hang-overs—the stubborn kid just *won't mind!*

"When're ya gonna get a *haircut,* for crying out loud!" yells Grandpa.

"Haircut? How'm I gonna be able to wear a ponytail if I get a haircut!" yells Ed.

The sale-priced washing machine arrived from Sears, Roebuck yesterday. The four of us spent an hour standing around the kitchen arguing over how to run it. Tina had one like it once, so she thought she knew everything.

"But Tina," I said, "it says in the book not to put the clothes in until the tub is full of water."

"Oh, never mind the book!" she says. (She has the same attitude about everything else, including the pressure cooker. "Tina, the book says when it hisses like that, there's something wrong." "Oh, never mind the book," she says.)

This washing machine has a wonderful invention attached to it called a wringer. You push a button and the dirty water pumps out of the tub and into the sink. You feed the clothes through the wringer, keeping in mind its propensity to bite the hand that feeds it. Then you go out in the yard, where the sun is shining and a breeze is blowing, and you dreamily hang up the clothes, feeling like a pioneer woman. After you've hung them up, you take them down again because you remember you forgot to rinse them. Never mind, it will be fun to match wits with the wringer again.

February 26, 1956
Cohasset, Massachusetts

This morning I could feel a bad mood coming on. As my dear ones will testify, when I get in a bad mood I should be put in a padded cell for the duration. Recently a more practical solution turned up in the form of some little pills recommended by Ed's company doctor. He claimed they were helpful in relieving tension.

Ed brought home a boxful last month, and when my nerves began to jangle, I started taking two a day. It may have been the power of suggestion, but they seemed to work. I became so gentle and patient with my children, they asked me what was the matter. My attitude toward Ed was one of such loving understanding, an outsider wouldn't have believed we were married. I faced the usual daily emergencies with good humor. To show his appreciation, Ed gave me a corsage of camellias on Valentine's Day. Instead of wanting to know what he'd been up to now, I thanked him. There was no getting around it, I was much nicer than I really am.

But now I lay in bed thinking black thoughts and refusing to resort to the Disposition Pills. Maybe they were habit-forming. It would be a terrible thing if I couldn't be agreeable without taking a pill first. All I needed was a little sleep.

I envied Ed the way he could sleep. The way he could sleep when I couldn't was grounds for divorce. I remembered my mother telling me that Dad sensed it when she had insomnia, no matter how careful she was not to disturb him. "What's the matter, honey bun? I can hear you thinking," he would say sympathetically.

When I have insomnia I could use a little husbandly sympathy myself. To make it easy for him, I don't even try to be quiet.

"Ho-hum," I said last night when the town clock struck 2:00. I upheaved my blankets and rolled over with a thump, hitting my head on the bookcase headboard. The door rattled along its track like the Toonerville trolley. Not a sound from Ed.

"Ouch!" I said lonesomely.

There was a soft snore from the bed next to mine, followed by a breezy sigh. He must be dreaming it's his birthday and he's blowing out the candles, I thought. Snore, puff, snore, puff, snore, puff.

I turned on the light and shone it on Eddie's face to see if he was pretending. Snore, puff. I read a few more chapters of *Marjorie Morningstar*. I reached the point where Marjorie was on the brink of an exciting career and losing her virginity. She was twenty-one. At twenty-one, where had *I* been? Out in the laundry, washing diapers for *his* children. What had my life been since then? More children and more diapers, and anyone who calls that an exciting career is a man.

I dropped *Marjorie Morningstar* on the floor and switched out the light. My exciting career was dreaming about girls. Sigh, wolf whistle, sigh, wolf whistle. I stabbed him in the back with my forefinger.

"Humph, flumph, hunh? Wassa matter, cancha sleep?"

"Aren't you the perceptive one! I haven't closed an eye for hours, if you're really interested."

"Z Z Z Z."

I look forward to sleeping late Sunday morning while the children get ready for Sunday school. This morning I wearily focused one eye on the clock and tried to make out the time without waking up. I heard Kathryn call from the foot of the stairs that it was after 8:30 and breakfast was nearly ready. If Vonnie would remember to rouse Teddy from his ivory tower on the third floor, I could go back to sleep. The harrowing thing is, sometimes she remembers and sometimes she doesn't. Remembering is only half the battle. Ted is like his father; he can sleep through *anything*, especially the hour before Sunday school. (On Saturdays he's up and dressed with no prodding; basketball practice starts at nine.)

I dragged myself from bed and called up to the third floor, "Teddy, are you up?"

"Yeh," came the sleepy answer.

"Well, come down and get dressed right away or you'll be late for Sunday school. Don't forget to make your bed."

I closed the windows and crawled back into bed. I waited for the sound of bare feet pounding down the stairs. Ten minutes later I got up and called him again.

"Yah, yah, I'm coming. You want me to make my bed, don't you?"

"Well, not from scratch, Teddy."

Back to bed. Bare feet pounded down the stairs and into Timmy's room, where the boys share a closet.

As time went by I knew I'd better check on their progress. I tapped on the door and looked in. Teddy was in Timmy's bed, snuggled under the covers. Timmy, in his underpants, was in the midst of a flying tackle.

I blew my top. "Okay, you two, if you're not ready to go downstairs in five minutes—teeth brushed, beds made, hair combed, faces washed—you're both going to bed early tonight."

"Don't we have to get dressed?" Timmy asked.

"I mean it, now! I'm sick and tired of going through this same nonsense week after week, two big boys like you, what are you, babies? Well, if you're babies, you can go to bed early like babies. From now on, either you kids are ready for breakfast at nine o'clock every Sunday or you go to bed early. Is that clear?"

As I stomped out of the room Teddy mumbled something and Timmy said loyally, "She is not!"

"*I'm* ready, Mummy," Vonnie called virtuously from the bathroom, where she was polishing her shoes.

"Oh, goody for you!" said Teddy.

"*Vonnie!*" I scolded. "That's not the right polish, look at the mess you're making, what are you doing with Daddy's polish?"

"I like to open the can."

"Honestly, Vonnie, what a mess. You've got little bits of polish all over the floor. You're *stepping* on it! No, don't use the good towel! Put the can away and use the polish in the bottle and *don't* spill it. Besides, why are you wearing your school shoes instead of your patent leathers?"

"Because my patent leathers don't need polishing," Vonnie said with patient eleven-year-old logic.

"Vonnie, some rainy day you can polish all the shoes in the house. Now go put on your patent leathers, Kathryn is calling you for breakfast."

"Hey, Mummy, I can't find any socks," Timmy said.

"There must be some in the laundry room. Take your shoes and go on downstairs before your breakfast gets cold."

"I'm having cold cereal," said Timmy, always ready for an argument.

"*Get going!!*"

Ed was awake when I returned to our room. "Honestly, those kids of yours are going to drive me out of my mind!" I said, glaring at him.

"Why don't you take a tranquilizer?"

"Take a *pill?* It's not me! It's those kids! They're irresponsible, inconsiderate, lazy, careless—"

"*Children.*"

I snatched open a bureau drawer and the handle fell off. "You *see?*"

"Take a pill," said Eddie.

Vonnie came in, carrying a pad of paper.

"What now, Vonnie," I sighed.

"I want to show you the picture I drew of you. I think it's the best picture I ever drew."

"Not now, go down and have your breakfast!"

"It'll only take a minute," she said, leafing through the pages. "Here it is—oh, no, that's not it, I'll find it in a minute."

"For *heaven's sake,* Vonnie!"

"Oh, here it is! It's a picture of you. Isn't it good?"

"Very good. Now run along."

She gave me a hug and ran downstairs. I looked at the picture again. Under it she had printed: "My mother is a beautiful picture to me."

I put down the picture and went to the medicine cabinet. I took two tranquilizers.

Breakfast might have been pleasant if I'd taken the pills sooner. I got our breakfast ready while Ed drove the children to Sunday school and picked up the papers. When he walked in, he threw his coat down on one of the dining room chairs.

He does this every night of the week. When I'm not in a bad mood, my thought process is as follows: "The poor, tired boy! He works so hard making a living for his family, he's too exhausted to hang up his coat. What a privilege it is for me to hang it in the closet for him!" I put the coat away with a tender smile of understanding. (I know I'm sincere about this because I don't wait for him to come downstairs and see how understanding I'm being.)

When I'm in a bad mood, there's nothing that irritates me more than this habit of throwing his coat on a chair. "For Pete's sake," I say to myself, "how am I supposed to train the children to be neat if their own father doesn't set them a good example! Suppose we *all* threw our coats on a chair, wouldn't the house look lovely! I'll bet it takes him longer to walk into the dining room and drop his coat than it would to open the hall closet and hang it up."

This morning, while ostentatiously transferring Ed's coat to the closet, I expressed these thoughts aloud. Eddie looked surprised and promised to set a good example hereafter.

Then there was the way he ate his grapefruit. Usually I don't notice the way he eats his grapefruit because I'm too busy tackling mine. But today I watched and listened with an air of distaste. Couldn't he take a spoonful without that silly gasp? He went after it as if someone were going to steal it from him. After slurping up the last section, he squeezed the grapefruit over the bowl, which he raised to his lips, gulping the juice with the gusto of a parched water buffalo.

"If you could *see* yourself!" I exploded. "Would you eat grapefruit that way if you were having breakfast with Marilyn Monroe?"

Ed looked thoughtful. "No," he said. "I'd have her feed it to me."

This afternoon when I found smears of liquid shoe polish on the bathroom rug, I summoned Vonnie.

"Look what you've done now!" I said. "Didn't I warn you not to spill it? No more polishing shoes for you until you learn not to be so sloppy."

"I *didn't* spill it."

I asked Timmy and Teddy if they had been using the polish.

"Not me," said Ted.

"Me either," said Timmy.

"*Well*, Vonnie? This rug didn't get smeared by itself."

"I didn't spill any, but—well—maybe it came off the bottom of my shoes."

"The *bottom* of your shoes?"

"Yes," she said, twisting one leg around the other. "I polished the bottoms."

Who but Vonnie would be inspired to polish the soles of her shoes? Wasn't it Vonnie who chewed gum until her jaw got stuck and she had to go to the doctor? Who sealed her lips with Scotch tape and then asked her father for a kiss? And at the tense point in the movie when the villainess dove from the float to recover the knife from her victim's back, wasn't it Vonnie who exclaimed: "She's a good diver!"

"You're a character, Vonnie," I said. Then I remembered something. I told her I loved the picture she drew of me, and I was going to have it framed.

October 1, 1959
Cohasset

For the first time in months and months I am alone in the house. Timmy will be home before long, but even an hour to myself is unique to the point of being precious. Kathryn is baby-sitting for Mrs. Tosi, and Mother and Vaughan are on their way to Vermont to visit Aunt Alma. There's no one around to ask questions or tell me something is wrong with the garbage disposal. Even the telephone is silent; all I can hear is the distant cacophony of gulls circling above the cove, the rustle of waves unfurling on the beach, and, under my nose, the scratch of pen on paper. Soothing, undemanding sounds . . .

A few days ago Kathryn complained that the cap for the bottom of the flour bin was missing. Taking a poll of the family, I tracked down the flour bin cap snatcher, Timothy. "It's upstairs on my desk," he said. "I'll bring it right down."

"May I ask what you were doing with it?" Ed asked with a certain wary curiosity.

"Oh, I was just doing a little experiment with some flour and a candle. You take a coffee can and punch a hole in it and put a rubber tube through the hole. Then you put a dish of flour inside the can and a candle next to it. You light the candle, put the top on the can, and blow through the tube."

"And then they cart you off to the bughouse?" I said.

"No, then you get this beautiful explosion," Tim explained, quite pleased with himself.

Ed looked at me and said numbly, "He could have blown up the whole house." I thought he was exaggerating, but he said even a small amount of flour under compression is a dangerous concoction.

I suppose someday when Tim is a famous nuclear physicist, we'll look back on this incident and laugh, if we're still in one piece.

August 17, 1960
Cohasset

Ed's mother is here for a few days. Mimi's faculty for getting on everyone's nerves, especially her son's, is undiminished. I think he is sharp with her because her constant chatter not only bores him but embarrasses him. He forgets that Mother, Vaughan, and the rest of us are able to be patient because we love *him.*

During dinner at the Cabin, Mimi kept apologizing for being such a slow eater. That's because her mouth was otherwise occupied. When she couldn't think of something new to say, she'd repeat in the same tedious detail whatever she had just finished telling us (the bargain hat she discovered at Gilchrist's, the wedding of her second cousin's daughter). I kept Edward on an even keel by nudging him gently under the table every now and then, so the evening went peaceably enough.

When we got home, Mimi stopped to chat with Kathryn in the kitchen, and Ed and I went on up to bed. He has had terrible cold sores for two weeks and has been as grouchy as a bear, and about as approachable. Now that his mouth is clearing up, he is more like himself—a wolf. (Rrrruff!) So we were cuddling, and I was catching up on the loving he owed me when we heard Mimi at the door.

"Barbara, are you awake?"

"No!" I said as convincingly as I could. In the same breath Ed snapped, "We're asleep, go away!"

"I brought up your bag, Barbara," Mimi said, turning the knob. "I thought you might like—"

"Leave it there, leave it there!" Ed said frantically.

"I don't need it right now, Mimi," I said. "Leave it on the shelf outside the door and I'll get it tomorrow."

"Oh. Well, all right. I hope I didn't wake you up. I just thought you might want—"

"Go away!" her son sobbed.

Poor Mimi! Poor Edward!

September 26, 1960
Cohasset

Our neighbor Don Morse called yesterday and wanted to know if we had anyone in the family who liked birds. Recognizing a trap question when I heard one, I said tentatively, "Well, there's our cat, Dizzy."

"Oh, I don't think your cat would be interested in tangling with this fellow. He's a big black crow and I can't persuade him to leave our porch. Don't know whether he's someone's pet or what. He can't fly, but he has a good appetite."

I told Don I would relay his message to Vonnie when she came in from riding.

"Who was that?" Ed asked.

"Don Morse has a tame crow he's *trying to get rid of,*" I said.

It was no use. Ed threw down the Sunday papers and rushed out to the back hall to get a carton. "Bring along some bread," he ordered, as I resignedly put on my jacket. "A tame crow! Imagine that! Maybe we can teach him to talk!"

Remembering the careless habits of a succession of pet sea gulls, I said I wouldn't be impressed until he learned to say "Which way to the bathroom?" I wanted to know who would be in charge of hosing the terrace *this* time.

"Why, you, of course!" Ed said, clapping me on the back. "You're so much better at it than the rest of us!"

"That kind of flattery will get you nowhere," I said.

Don was delighted to see us. "The crow was at the front door just a minute ago," he said, pointing to the evidence. "I think he's half-starved."

"I think he has diarrhea," I said.

Following the spoor, we found the bird strutting around on the side porch.

"Hello, hello," I croaked encouragingly. His guttural response might have been intelligible to a fellow crow, but he'd have been a flop on TV.

"See if he'll eat the bread," said Ed.

I tossed him a crust, which disappeared down his black gullet in a flash. Gradually I lured him toward me with strategically dropped crumbs of bread.

"Now put the box over him," I said to Ed.

"I'm afraid it might scare him to death. Why don't you just grab him?"

I looked dubious. "If he bites, it won't hurt much," he said.

"*You* grab him," I said.

"But he *knows* you," Ed argued. "You're the one that's been feeding him."

"Here you are." I relinquished the bread and folded my arms. "Good luck."

"Here, fella, here, fella," Ed said ingratiatingly, extending a piece of bread. The crow looked him over and backed up a few steps. Ed dropped the crust and, when the crow sidled up to it, made a grab for him. He was quick, but so was the crow. Ed chased him all over the porch, swooping down and coming up with one handful of air after another. Finally he succeeded in cornering the rascal. What a caw-motion!

"Ow!" said Ed, as his captive hacked away at his fetters (Ed's fingers).

"Does it hurt?" I asked solicitously.

We walked back to the house by way of the beach because Ed was afraid automobiles might alarm his friend. His friend, meanwhile, was attempting to chop his hand off at the wrist, an operation Ed endured with a minimum of plaintive ow's.

The question was, Where to keep the creature until he overcame his aversion to human society and his craving for human flesh? Since we had spent the morning cleaning the garage, I was opposed to shutting him in there. The floor was so clean and neat, for the first time in years, I had been thinking of putting up a sign: "Do Not Enter Without Removing Shoes."

"How about the barn?" said Ed. "That's a mess, anyway."

We put the crow in the barn and left a note on the door so Vonnie and Heidi wouldn't be taken by surprise when she got home from her ride.

Vonnie was enchanted with her new pet. She named him Ajax and at the moment is busily making a cage for him out of chicken wire.

Later

Vonnie is crushed. She finished the cage but then found to her sorrow that Ajax had turned up his heels and died. Poor fellow! I guess Ed disagreed with him.

October 14, 1960
Cohasset

When I was shopping at Tedeschi's yesterday, a voice came over the loudspeaker asking the owner of a black Ford convertible (I had Ed's car, so I pricked up my ears), license number H666, to come to the courtesy desk.

"Maybe it's something pleasant," I thought, "like 'Because you are our one millionth customer, we are giving you a new Thunderbird, this full-length mink coat, and a trip to Paris!'"

Au contraire. The man at the courtesy desk told me I had parked my car in such a way that the car beside it was blocked. An agitated woman was waiting for me in the parking lot. Her car had just been painted, and she hoped I could back out successfully, although she doubted it because our fenders were practically touching, and how had I managed to park so close without scraping her fender she couldn't imagine.

I moved the Ford to the tune of gasps, squeals, and prayers emanating from this bundle of nerves and returned to the store. I was looking for the family-size packages of English muffins when a man tapped me on the shoulder and said I had made off with his basket. Perhaps I'd prefer mine, which I had left yonder at the end of the aisle.

To round out the day, Edward was mean to me. He was preparing to finish a repair job he'd begun on the bathroom light last weekend. "Of course you saved that little nut I left in the globe," he said.

I said, "You mean that tiny weeny roundish thing?"

"You *didn't* throw it away!"

I allowed as how I might have. I remembered hearing something drop when I picked up the globe to wash it. It was possible I might have tossed out whatever it was in the basket.

"Oh, this urge to clean," Ed said. "How am I going to fix this damn thing now, tell me that! You women and your urge to clean!"

He stomped out of the kitchen and I yelled after him, "What do you mean, urge to clean, I have no urge to clean and it's a good thing I don't or I couldn't live in this house, why didn't you fix that light six months ago when I first asked you to, boy, I wonder how many women could stand living in a house where things don't get fixed for years!"

After I'd simmered down a bit I remembered it was his birthday and he was going to take me out to dinner. I decided to forgive him as soon as I could without losing face.

I was reading the paper when I heard him come and stand behind me in a way I could tell was repentant. He didn't say anything, so I didn't say anything, not wanting to lose face. Then he started upstairs. Mustering a pleasant tone of voice, I called, "How's it going?"

"Oh, fine!" he said, sounding startled.

When he came down again he said with a grin, "Guess what! I'm smarter than I thought I was. When I took that fixture apart last weekend, I remember I said to myself, 'If I leave this nut where the nut I married can get her hands on it, she'll throw it away.' So I screwed it into the rim, and there it was when I looked for it."

Ed had insisted that I shouldn't get anything for his birthday because we couldn't afford it, but I wanted him to have *something* to open, even if it was made of plastic and cost a dollar and a half. I gave him his present and told him we were going to play twenty questions.

Ed put down his paper and took up the challenge.

"One: is it something for the boat?"

"Yes."

"Aha!" said he. "You never thought I'd get there *that* fast, did you!"

After several more questions he established that it was something you would use in an emergency, not necessarily at night, and although it felt like a cranberry scoop, it was not a cranberry scoop. (I had told him *not* to feel it, but the closer he got to the twentieth question, the more he cheated.)

I gave him a hint. "What is the biggest emergency we could possibly have on the boat? *Think!*"

"We're sinking," he said.

"Right."

"An inflatable life preserver!" he said.

"Cranberry scoop was closer."

In the end he gave up and tore off the wrappings.

"Oh, for heaven's sake!" he said. "I thought it was something *expensive!*"

"You told me *not* to get something expensive!"

"I didn't know you'd take me up on it. Well, it's a very nice bailer."

December 12, 1960
Cohasset

A northeast blizzard rattled the house during the night. Ed started for work and got stuck in Quincy along with hundreds of other stranded motorists. He spent the day sitting in a nearby drugstore and has just phoned me that he's going to set out to the Marshes' house—half an hour's walk, he figures. It is bitterly cold out, so I'm worried about him.

There was no school today. Tim called from Providence to tell me there was no school at Moses Brown, either.* He said he had ripped his good trousers, but he thought they could be mended. How did he tear them? "Sliding down a banister."

Later

While I was having dinner with Mom and Kathryn, I reported that the man of the house was walking through the storm to the Marshes'. I added that I wouldn't be worried if it weren't so cold.

"The biggest danger is stepping on live wires in the dark," said Kathryn.

I hadn't thought of that, but now I could think of nothing else. At last Ed called. He had reached the Marshes' house safely, having run all the way, he said, to keep his feet from freezing.

I was taking a shower a little before nine when Vonnie tapped on the door and said Ed was on the phone. I wrapped a towel around me and dripped downstairs to talk to him. (Mom was sitting beside our bedroom phone, watching TV— the downstairs sets weren't working.) Ed said he missed me; more so than when he was out of town because we were so frustratingly close to each other. He'd talked to the local po-

---

* Moses Brown is a Quaker boarding school, attended by Ed in the thirties and also by Ted, who graduated in June 1960.

lice and learned the roads in Quincy were fairly navigable. He repeated that he missed me. He told me not to do anything foolish like trying to get him . . . Marion had a spare bed.

"Suppose I got stuck," I said.

"Yes, you might. You just stay put, don't try to come after me."

"If the situation were reversed, you'd come after me," I said.

"I'm a big strong man, and you're a silly, weak, helpless, adorable female."

Once again he urged me not to do anything foolish, and I hung up convinced that something foolish was what he wanted me to do.

I bundled up, put on my boots, and hurried outdoors. A huge drift covered the front porch and there was a ten-inch layer of snow on the car. The window on the driver's side was open an inch, so I found the seat occupied by an abominable snowman. Even the steering wheel and the dashboard were covered with snow.

I finally got going but bogged down a few yards from the end of the driveway. When I tried the back-and-forward-dash technique a few times, the car began to act strangely, stalling and dimming its lights when I pressed on the starter.

I had to give up, but no one can say I didn't *try* to do something foolish.

December 14, 1960
Cohasset

Ed came home last night in a raunchy mood after being blizzarded in at the Marshes' on Monday night. He went to refresh his drink during a commercial and called out matter-of-factly from the bar that as soon as the movie we were watching, *Harvey,* was over, he'd like to go upstairs and cuddle. I flinched, not because I don't like cuddling, but because I knew Mom was watching TV in the playroom, within easier hearing distance of his proposition than I was.

"Shh, not in front of Mother!" I whispered with a frown, as he returned to the living room.

"Of course not!" he said, looking shocked. "Upstairs in bed was what I had in mind."

I wigwagged desperately in the direction of the playroom. Edward stopped stirring his drink and asked me with an air of mystification what I was doing—thumbing a ride or something?

By this time I was sure Mother was finding Ed much more interesting to listen to than *Harvey*. To express my mortification, I had a mild seizure, which involved sinking down in my chair until I was almost horizontal, flinging my arms wide, and rolling my eyes at the ceiling.

"That's it!" Ed cried. "*Now* you've got the idea!"

February 3, 1961
Cohasset

We went to the Red Lion with the Hills last night. Ed started ordering vodka martinis, so *I* decided to have vodka martinis. I find that if I stay a step ahead of him, he worries so much about my disgracing myself that he forgets to gulp his own drinks. This may be a far, far better thing I do than I have ever done, but it is not a far, far better rest I go to. Ed helped me upstairs, pulled off my sweater and skirt, tucked me into my cradle. I call it a cradle because who ever heard of a bed rocking?

I got up during the night and made the mistake of glancing in the mirror. My eyes were still made up, but the whites were the color of a Bloody Mary. I scrubbed my face, removing skin along with my fossilized lipstick. Then I peeled off the rest of my clothes, put on my nightie, and crawled back into my cradle.

This morning I was awakened by a quiet chuckle. I pried open my good eye and saw my husband standing with his hands on his hips, surveying something on the floor.

"What's funny?"

"Your clothes," he said. "They're all over the floor. Tsk tsk."

"Listen," I said, getting up on one elbow. "You shouldn't drink those vodka martinis, they're deadly!"

"*I* shouldn't drink vodka martinis!" said he, stupefied. "*I* was perfectly sober last night. I was in complete control of myself right up to the end!"

"Yes, dear, but there *have* been occasions—," I reminded him gently. "Really, I don't know why you drink those things, you're just asking for trouble!"

Ed shook his head dazedly. "You're a tough baby!" he said. "How this conversation has worked around to a discussion of *my* crimes is something I'll never be able to figure out."

"Don't forget to leave my check," I said, kindly changing the subject.

Ed was still shaking his head when he left the room.

February 17, 1961
Cohasset

I am discouraged about our poodle puppy. Her personal habits are getting worse instead of better—I'm beginning to wonder if Tokay isn't as bright as she looks. I'm no longer keen about breeding her unless we can move to Florida and raise the puppies on terrazzo floors.

I have another problem. Between Tokay's diet and Vaughan's diet, the refrigerator is as crammed with tidbits as it is in the summer, when everyone is home.* While I was rinsing the

* Kathie was a junior at Swarthmore College, Ted a freshman at Colby. Tim, heartily disliking boarding school, would pack up and leave two months later.

dishes Tuesday night, Ed began withdrawing various mysterious (to him) odds and ends from the shelves and making throwing-away motions.

"Don't throw that away!" I said. "That's Tokay's liver juice! I use it to flavor her vegetables."

Ed distastefully replaced the cover, then asked if it was necessary to have three different containers of butter. I said yes, it was, because one of them was Big Vaughan's butter, which was unsalted; one of them was Vonnie's butter, which I buy her occasionally as a treat; and the other was oleomargarine for us proletarians.

"Oh," said Ed. "Well, how about this gooey stuff? Whatever it is, don't feed it to me!"

"Egg whites left over from Tokay's egg yolks," I said. "Kathryn will make a lemon meringue pie sometime."

"And this odd-looking concoction?"

"Leftover vegetables for Tokay."

"Looks like garbage to me. What the devil's in here?" Ed said, pinching a limp foil-wrapped package. "Feels like a couple of boneless fingers."

"That's asparagus for my lunch. Stop squeezing it," I said. I was beginning to be annoyed because only that morning I had defrosted the refrigerator and disposed of enough moldering remains to stock a penicillin factory.

"And what's this mess here?" he persisted, sticking his nose into another container.

For a minute he had me stumped, but a gingerly taste convinced me it was last Saturday's oatmeal. "I'll have it for breakfast," I said.

"If this oatmeal isn't gone by tomorrow night," Edward said, "out it goes!"

"Is that so!" I said.

"Yes, that's so!" he said. "Let's have a little efficiency around here."

I had two choices: I could throw something at him or I could think of something. I thought of something.

"Listen," I said, "seeing as you're in such an industrious mood, how about going out to the playroom and cleaning the aquarium. It's a sight, and you promised me when you had that aquarium built into the wall that you'd keep it clean, the only one who ever cleans it is my mother, suppose someday she falls off the stool and breaks a leg, she isn't getting any younger, you know, what's the point of having an aquarium if—"

"Okay, okay, I'll clean it over the weekend," Ed said, backing out of the kitchen.

"How can you, we'll be up in Maine! I'm having two tables of bridge next week and I'm ashamed to have my friends see that aquarium, it's a disgrace, the fish can't see out and we can't see in!"

"I'll do it tomorrow night," Ed called.

Wednesday night, when I reminded him of his chore, he said he didn't think he had the proper cleaning tools; he'd bring some home the next night. I remembered that this is what he says whenever I try to pin him down on cleaning the aquarium.

"What did you do with the gadget you brought home last time, throw it away?"

"Gee, I guess it got lost or something," Ed said, settling down with the paper.

I rummaged around in the cupboards behind the bar and found the scraper tucked into a back corner. This is the kind of efficiency Edward doesn't admire.

Since it took him only five minutes to scrape the sides of the tank, I don't know what all the fuss was about. The fish seemed glad to see us and wagged their fins as if to say, "By Neptune, what a long night *that* was!"

February 20, 1961
Cohasset

Last night Ed read an article in the new *Journal* entitled "Should You Remarry a Man You've Divorced?" The idea apparently intrigued him because he brought it up two or three times during the evening. Blake Thaxter has always maintained that once people get a divorce they want no part of each other, but Ed doesn't visualize things that way.

"What I would do," he said thoughtfully as we were having dinner at the Cabin, "is come to see you a couple of times a week. No evil intentions, you understand—this would be just a friendly, platonic visit."

"You'd better call me first," I said. "I might be out."

"I'd bring you a little present of some kind: flowers, perfume, candy—"

"Just say money and I'll make a point of staying at home."

"I'd probably bring a clean shirt and socks so I could shower and change . . ."

"Not in *my* bathroom, you don't," I said. "That sounds entirely too domestic to me."

"All right, I'd go to my apartment and freshen up there—but you understand we'd lose a lot of time."

"You should have thought of that before the divorce."

"Okay, so you open the door and there I am. Let's see, what do you do? We're civilized people, you probably lean over and give me a little kiss on the cheek."

"Never!"

"Well, what *would* you do—shake hands?"

"I'd lean over and take the present and I'd say, 'You *know* I don't eat candy!'"

"Then we'd sit down and have a friendly little vodka martini . . ."

"I hope you brought your own. I've turned the bar into a Health Nook."

"I'd ask how the kids were—"

"You should know. You've got 'em!"

"—and Vaughan and your mother," he went on, undaunted.

"Vaughan's teaching calisthenics at the Community Center and Mother's earning good money house painting. You don't think we're getting along on your *alimony!*"

"Then I'd say, 'Where would you like to go to dinner—the Red Coach? Fox and Hounds? The Cabin?'"

"Oh, these decisions!"

"All right, I'd sweep you off your feet and order a candlelit table for two at the Florence Club—"

"You're reaching me—"

"I'd play 'our song' on the jukebox—"

"'Too Young,'" I said dreamily.

"Mildred would say, 'Mr. and Mrs. Malley, we haven't seen you in a *long* time!'"

"You'd hold my coat and open the door for me—"

"We'd stop at the beach to look at the moon—"

I took his hand and gazed into his eyes. "Let's go home and pretend we got married again."

May 15, 1961
Cohasset

Our dinner party Saturday night went off very well. I wore a new dress, an Empire style in pleated pale lavender wool, with a matching sweater. It's a becoming outfit; in fact, Gene Porta, who ordinarily looks right through me, being a bosom man, attributed my vanquishing him at Ping-Pong to my "sexy dress."

The nicest compliment came from Don Kneale, a houseguest staying with Daisy and Bill Rogers. He said I was one of the rare people he had ever met who had true maturity. He said this not once but twice, repeating it late in the evening when I am not always my most mature.

The lavender dress was the secret, I realized. It was a talisman that gave me poise and assurance. In order to perpetuate this illusion, all I had to do was wear it morning, noon, and night.

I woke up the next morning with a smile, remembering Don's compliment. Somewhere in this world was a person who thought I was mature. How very flattering. No one had ever said that about me before!

Ed heard me telling Mother about the lavender dress and its magical effect. "I'll buy her *thirty* lavender dresses!" he muttered.

May 16, 1961
Cohasset

I called Ed yesterday morning to remind him to pick up his mother at Columbia Circle.

"I can't pick her up," he said. "I'm going to Worcester, so I'll be late tonight. Do you want to put her off a week?"

"No, I'll do it."

Mimi was waiting for me on the steps of the rooming house when I arrived at five. I was hoping to get on the expressway before the heavy commuter traffic developed, but it was hard to pay attention to what I was doing. Mimi's tongue was drowning me in a stream of consciousness that would make James Joyce sound laconic. I got lost twice, took an hour and a half to get home, and was a nervous wreck by the time I pulled into the driveway. I could hardly wait for Ed to arrive, fix us a cocktail, help me listen to Mimi, and take us out to dinner.

"When will Edward be home?"

"He had to go to Worcester, so he'll probably be a little late."

At 7:15 Ed called. "Did you get my mother?"

"Oh, yes, she's here." I was pleased with myself for not getting upset. It was clear Ed would not be home before eight. Daisy and Bill's friend would have been proud of me for not flying off the handle the way some wives would.

"Well, I'd better run along now, the fellows are waiting."

"*Fellows?* What fellows? Where *are* you, anyway?"

"I'm in Worcester, where'd you think I was? I told you I was going to be late."

I should have rushed upstairs and put on my maturity dress. Instead I spilled out a torrent of protests that must have made his mother, who was scanning the paper nearby, assume divorce was around the corner.

"I thought you meant late for *dinner!* You didn't say *one word* about not being here for dinner!"

"You should have known—"

"Why should I have known? You don't always stay to dinner! Only the other morning you went to Worcester and didn't stay to dinner. When you said you were going to be late, I thought you meant too late to pick up your mother. I thought the three of us would be going out to dinner the way we always do!"

Ed said there was nothing he could do about it now. Even without the lavender dress I could see that his statement had logic.

Hanging up, I sat there for a minute with my hand on the receiver. How was I going to stand that voice for three more hours? I pulled myself together, explained to Mimi that I had misunderstood about Ed's plans, and asked if she'd like something to drink.

"You know, Barbara," she said with a pleased smile as I brought her a cocktail, "I had a strong premonition Edward wasn't going to be here tonight."

I believe in having respect for older people, but when she said that, I longed to pour the scotch and soda down the back of her neck. There is something about Mimi's premonitions that exasperates me beyond words. She never foresees anything pleasant. It's always something horrible like one of us getting burned or drowned or not coming home to dinner.

By the time I finished my drink I had resolved to be patient and make the best of things. To my surprise, Mimi and I had the most agreeable evening we've ever had. We went to the Lighthouse, and Mimi did all the talking, but it was interesting. She told me about the cruise she took one summer when Ed was in camp. The carved chest in Kathie's room was one of the treasures she bought in Hong Kong; large objects like this were delivered to the ship free of charge. She got one chest for Ed and one for herself. She also brought back a couple of Oriental rugs.

"Some of the women spent their tourist allowance so foolishly, but I took my time and bought only the best."

Poor Mimi, she *does* try, but the one thing she's never tried since I've known her is to stop talking for a while.

December 25, 1961
Fort Lauderdale

While normal people gathered together on Christmas Eve to sing carols around the old TV set, little did I guess what I would be getting myself into—a racing machine known as a go-cart.

Earlier this week Ted had gone to the track with a friend. Next to flying, he told us, go-carting was the world's greatest thrill, and he wouldn't rest until his father and Tim tried it.

I had no intention of joining the men in their quaint suicidal sport. My preference was to stay home alone and read (the girls were out on a double date), but the fellows wouldn't hear of it. Come along and watch, they insisted. If you get bored you can read your book.

We drove to the go-cart arena, and the next thing I knew, Ed was thrusting a ticket in my hand and urging me to share in the fun.

"But I just wanted to watch!" I bleated, as he herded me along toward the track.

"Be a sport, kid," he coaxed. "You don't have to go fast. Any time it seems to be getting away from you, just take your foot off the gas."

The appeal to be a sport never fails to reach me and usually gets me in a peck of trouble. Pushing thoughts of possible mutilation to the back of my mind, I approached the nearest go-cart.

"Don't take that red one, Mom," Ted warned, "that's one of the fast ones."

So they had minds of their own, like horses! If you didn't keep the upper hand, would they put down their heads and take off for Key West? "I think I'd rather watch," I said.

"Oh, come on, Maw, don't be chicken," Tim said.

"She isn't chicken, she just isn't as young as she used to be," Ted said. "Isn't that right, Mom?"

That did it. I allowed myself to be led to one of the less spirited carts. As I lowered myself onto the seat, I resolved to stop complaining about the difficulty of getting in and out of Ed's Austin-Healy. It, at least, was knee-high. This contraption was nothing more than a wheelbase with a seat in the middle, and once you were in it, you were practically sitting on the ground.

Directly in front of me was a pedal on my left that said

"brake" and a pedal to the right that said "gas." These were located so close to the seat that when I placed my feet on them, there was nowhere for my knees to go but out. I sat there looking like a grasshopper with skirts on, realizing with a blush that I should be wearing shorts.

The track attendant hunched down and explained how to run the cart, but I was too busy trying to make my skirt into a culotte to hear much of what he said.

The men had already stepped on the gas and were speeding down the straightaway toward the first curve. I pushed the pedal down a fraction of an inch, and *zoooom*, I was hurtling toward the curve at a hell-bent pace. These beasts had two speeds, I found, top and neutral. I had my choice between zooming or stopping and getting trampled under the wheels of the charioteers roaring up behind me.

Before I had time to make a decision, *zoom, zoom, zoom*—the three speed demons screamed past me, enveloping me in a cloud of dust. All three gave me a patronizing smile and a wave.

After I stopped choking, I again applied the tiniest amount of pressure to the gas pedal, and negotiated the first curve on two wheels. I was expecting the hairpin bend, but not the curlicue that confronted me. Curve after curve materialized in split-second succession, their circumferences outlined by stacks of gaily painted tires. Leaving the stacks less tidy than they were before I came along, I jerked and bumped my way around the first lap. Then my engine quit. I stepped on the pedal warily, to make sure it wasn't just playing dead; then I pumped it, but there was still no response.

Eddie swerved around me, yelling, "What's the matter, kid, are you stalled?"

"No, Dum-Dum, I just stopped to look at a road map," I muttered.

Tim, whose view of my problem had been blocked by his father, was bearing down the stretch wide open. As he saw me, his eyebrows shot up into his crew cut. Slamming on the brakes, he turned his wheel hard left. He missed me, but sent several painted tires flying.

I saw the attendant stride purposefully toward me. "I'll have you going in a jiffy," he said. He cranked up my engine or wound up my spring or some damn thing, and I was back in the rat race. Around and around I went, trying to control my ballooning skirt with one hand and avoid collisions with the other. I felt like a character out of Dante's inferno and decided that if Hell was anything like this, I was going to mend my ways.

At last the young man stepped to the edge of the track and signaled with a checkered flag that the ordeal was over. I felt like saluting it. While I crawled out and tested my legs to see if I was doomed to be known henceforth as the Grasshopper Lady, the boys purchased another round of tickets. Wouldn't I like to try it again now that I had the hang of it?

This marks one of the few times that I've turned down the chance to be a good companion to my husband. I said no, thank you, and returned to my book reading. That's more my speed.

January 15, 1962
Cohasset

As we were leaving the house Friday afternoon, Ed slowed the car near the end of the driveway and said in a brisk, businesslike tone, "Now, are you sure you've remembered everything? Toothbrushes? Toothpaste? Cards? Cameras?"

"Pajamas?" I said.

I've never forgotten the fuss he made one summer night when he found he had no pajamas on the boat. I had brought them home to be laundered the previous weekend and neglected to replace them. He carried on as if I'd dropped his charge cards overboard.

"Pajamas?" he muttered with a look of mild panic, jamming on the brakes. Then he relaxed and said he was sure he'd packed them.

After dinner in the main building at Eastover, we drove to our quarters. Ed read the evening paper while I unpacked, then we went for a walk around the grounds and explored the facilities. We decided the rest of the guests could have the ski slope and the skating rink; we'd settle for the indoor pool. We had a couple of drinks at the Tally-Ho, watched the young folks doing the twist, resisted the hamburger counter, which was doing a flourishing business as we left, and returned to our room.

Ed prepared a Small Libation to Play Cards By while I got into something comfortable, a pretty new pink negligee. My old blue corduroy was comfortable, too, but not whistle-provoking.

Ed whistled and said, "*That* must have cost a pretty penny!"

That's the way it goes after twenty-two years.

"What did you do with my pajamas?" Ed asked, as I sat down on the bed and began shuffling the cards.

"I didn't do anything with them. I don't remember seeing them when I unpacked."

"You *must* have seen them! Now stop and think, what did you do with them—did you hang them in the closet or put them in the drawer?"

"Are you sure you packed them?"

"Of *course* I packed them!" He upheaved socks, neckties, and underwear as he ransacked his drawer.

"Don't get so excited," I said. "You can always buy another pair tomorrow."

"But what am I gonna do *tonight*?"

I have never known a man who was so helpless without his pajamas. I'm not an expert on men in pajamas or men *not* in pajamas, but common sense tells me a fellow ought to be able to survive a pajama-less night without injury to the psyche. If Marilyn Monroe can slumber in nothing but Chanel No. 5, why couldn't my husband make do with a dab of Old Spice?

"They *must* be *somewhere!*" he was saying, turning the suitcase upside down.

"Why don't you wear your shorts?"

"But my legs would be bare!" he whimpered. "I get goose pimples!"

"I'm not asking you to be presented at court, all you have to do is get into bed. It's simple! Put on your shorts and *pretend* they're pajamas."

Ed wasn't listening. He was busily raking through *my* clothes, which I had neatly folded away in *my* drawer.

"What are these?" he demanded, holding up a red undergarment.

"Those are my tights," I said, eyeing him warily as he dangled them in front of him.

"They *were* your tights," he corrected me. "As of this moment they're *my pajamas.*"

"Oh, no!" I said, clapping my hand over my mouth.

Pleased with his ingenuity, Ed began working himself into my tights. He reminded me of a movie I'd seen of a snake shedding its skin, only the process was reversed. He tugged and pulled and twisted and stretched until he finally got the thing above his knees. I had lost my fight to keep a straight face and was doubled up on the bed, gasping, "You'd be a sensation in a fire drill." He paid me no more heed than would your molting python. As he squirmed and wriggled and yanked, the elastic waistband gradually approached his middle. He was making progress, no doubt about it.

Patiently he began again at his ankles, stretching the nylon toward his knees with both hands; working his way upward, he at last accumulated enough material to cover his navel. Standing back, he surveyed himself in the mirror over the bureau.

"*Now* I will put on my shorts," he decided, pulling a pair of striped drawers over the tights. I broke up again.

Looking like a cross between a demented Romeo and a giant two-legged red spider, my husband poured us another small libation and proposed a friendly game of rummy.

"For once I'm going to beat you at your own game!" he said, dealing seven cards apiece with a flourish.

It was my unlucky night. In spite of being distracted by the outlandish appearance of my opponent, I *couldn't* lose, no matter how I tried. With every hand, my Romeo became glummer. When I drew the eight of hearts, which filled a run, gave me a hundred extra points, put me out, and made me the winner for the fourth time in a row—well, under the circumstances, even a good loser might be forgiven a modest display of temper. From my husband, who is known neither for his modesty nor his good-loser-ship, I expected a display that would send the people of Massachusetts running for their root cellars.

Either he was unusually self-controlled or the tights had an inhibiting influence. All he did was throw the cards across the room and snarl, "It must be nice to be so damn lucky!"

"You're perfectly right, honey," I said, rescuing some of the nearer cards. "Drawing the eight of hearts was nothing but pure luck."

"That's right, *gloat*, go ahead and *gloat!*" Ed crawled into bed, pulled the covers up over his head, and that was the last I saw of him until morning.

The next day he made a Malley-type apology for his behavior of the night before. He came up behind me while I was

brushing my hair, gave me a hug, and said, "There's one wonderful thing about me, whenever I play cards it doesn't matter
a bit to me who wins or loses."

"Yeah," I sniffed, "—as long as the one who wins is you."

"Who, *me?*" he said with pained innocence.

After breakfast we tried out the hairpin curve toboggan a
couple of times, and that was the extent of our participation
in winter sports. The rest of the weekend we spent gravitating
between the pool and the Finnish sauna room. The first time
Ed lured me into the sauna room, I felt as if I were inhaling
fire, and ran out gasping for air. He gave me a lecture, pointing
out that if so many people enjoyed sitting around in super-
heated air, steaming the poisons out of their systems, there
must be something to it. So I gave it another try, and managed
to stand the heat for ten or fifteen minutes. I didn't *enjoy*
it, the way Edward does; I *endured* it. The things I do for
togetherness!

Saturday night we learned that the hamburgers we had by-
passed the previous evening were free. We couldn't wait to
rush over to the Tally-Ho and cram down hamburgers on top
of dinner. Big thick juicy hamburgers with onions and pickles
and coleslaw—free!

Ed and I woke up yesterday morning feeling as if we had
swallowed basketballs. We couldn't go without breakfast,
though; we were paying for a six-meal weekend. So a huge
breakfast went down to join the basketballs—it's a wonder
we didn't dent the bottom of the pool when we jumped in. We
swam, we steamed, but it was no use; by noontime we still felt
like Tweedledum and Tweedledee. Paid for or not, those slabs
of roast beef on the dining room buffet were not for us. We
checked out and drove home.

January 29, 1962
Cohasset

We went up to Colby to watch Ted play hockey Saturday afternoon. After the game we took Ted and his roommate out to dinner, then went on our way. We planned to stop at a motel within an hour or so of home, leaving us an easy drive the next day. When we got to New Hampshire, we decided on Lamie's Tavern, for nostalgic reasons. Hampton was the town where we were married just after I turned eighteen.

Yesterday morning we were having breakfast when Ed said, "I wonder what's happened to Mr. Penniman. He sure seemed uneasy about marrying us!"

"Let's look him up in the telephone book. If he's still around, why don't we drop in and reassure him?"

The only Penniman in Hampton was listed under Penniman Insurance Agency. It might not be the same fellow, but having gone this far on our sentimental journey, we couldn't give up now. After getting directions, we drew up in front of the same old white farmhouse where we had pledged our troth twenty-two years ago.

A pleasant-looking lady with her hair in curlers came to the door.

"Mr. Penniman hasn't been here for a good many years," she said. "Can I help you?"

"Well, we were wondering"— I looked uncertainly at Ed— "you see, this Mr. Penniman was a justice of the peace, and we were hoping he'd still be here."

The lady looked at me and then at Ed. "I'm a justice of the peace," she said with an encouraging smile.

"The reason we particularly wanted to see Mr. Penniman," I explained, "was because he married us when we were very young. We'd eloped, you see, and we wanted to tell him everything turned out all right."

"We have four children," Ed said. "Two of them in college."

"Isn't that nice!" beamed the lady.

"Is Mr. Penniman—not living?" I asked.

"Oh, he's very much alive! He's been up before the justice two or three times himself!"

"You mean—he's been *married* two or three times?"

"Yes indeed! He's living up in Maine with his third wife. I was the *first* Mrs. Penniman."

"Then you were one of our witnesses! Of course you wouldn't remember, but you asked the couple next door to come over and be witnesses, too. Mr. Penniman told us to remember it was easier to tie the knot than to untie it."

"He didn't practice what he preached, did he! But tell me your name and I'll relay your message. Once in a great while I do hear from him."

Ed and I gamely took pictures of the house and each other, but we agreed that our romantic gesture had been a bit of a fizzle.

February 12, 1962
Cohasset

Ed got up early and put another blanket on the bed.

"Thank you," I said. "I was too frozen to move. What time is it?"

"Five-thirty. Remind me to tell you about the dream I had when we get up."

"I had wild dreams, too. It must have been something we ate."

When I next awoke it was 7:15. I was upset to discover that Tim was finishing one of his interminable showers, and Vonnie was still asleep.

"You two should be downstairs eating your breakfast this very minute! Why didn't you get Vonnie up when your alarm went off? Now she'll have to rush off to school without a thing to eat, that's the second time this week!"

"Relax, Maw," Tim said. "How long does it take to eat a scrambled egg?"

"Timmy, you know how long it takes her to get ready! By the time she finishes combing her hair the bus will be here— she should have been up half an hour ago!"

"Don't worry about it, Maw!"

"Don't worry about it, don't worry about it," I muttered. I returned to my bed and lay there brooding about the irresponsibility of teenagers. Ed reached over and caressed my head.

"That dream I had was so vivid," he said. "It was back when we were young. . . ."

He paused for a moment and I said, "Well, go on—did I or didn't I?"

"We forget," he said. "We take things for granted. In the dream you were Barbara Beyer again—and boy, did I want to marry you!"

"It must have been the corned beef and cabbage."

"You didn't want to, though. I tried everything I could think of to persuade you, but you weren't—well, you weren't *gonna*, that's all. We were intimate, there was no doubt about that, but you'd reached the stage where you were talking about a platonic relationship, so I wasn't very happy about that."

"Well, as long as I just *talked* about it—"

"Lord, how it took me back! You were very sweet and nice, but you just didn't want to marry me. I kept trying to figure out ways of getting you pregnant—"

"There's more than one way?"

"—so you'd *have* to marry me. You seemed like the most desirable creature in the world, you were exactly as you were when I first met you: tall, slim, willowy—"

"Instead of short, fat, and dumpy the way I am now?"

"—your eyes were bright and sparkling—"

"*These* dull, lusterless things?"

"You were charming and pert—"

"Hey, *Maw,* whadja do with those trousers I asked you to sew?"

"—and carefree," I sighed. "Try looking in your *closet,*" I called.

Tim's sliding door clattered and screeched as he looked in the closet. "Oh, yeah," he said. "Hey, is Dad up? I want to get there early, you know."

"Be right with you, Tim." Ed jumped out of bed and began hurrying into his clothes. I brushed my teeth, bathed my eyes with cold water until they sparkled, combed my hair. My poor, rejected hubby! If he asked me to marry him, I was going to say yes.

I was waiting expectantly by the door when there came a rap. Tim came in to get his allowance and told his father to hurry up, it was getting late.

"Won't even have time to eat my grapefruit!" Ed grumbled.

"Why do you cater to him? It's his own fault for standing under the shower all morning. Take your time!"

"Come on, Dad," Tim called.

"He likes to go down to Braintree Center and have a cup of coffee with his buddies," Ed said, giving me a peck on the cheek.

"Is that all I get after that dream?" I said with a pout.

"Stick around," he said.

But I know what will happen. Long before he comes home he'll have forgotten about the elusive siren of his dreams and I'll be available old me again.

I wonder if he'd go for corned beef and cabbage two nights in a row?

Three

Malley's Madhouse
(1959–1965)

Yup, "Malley's Madhouse" was the affectionate term we used for our domicile as the kids were growing up. Hah! We didn't know what madness was until we were confronted by a phenomenon known as adolescence.

September 15, 1959
Cohasset, Massachusetts
To Kathie Malley

Dear Kathie:
One of my favorite people went away and left me "all-alonesome" (an expression of yours, many years ago). You, my darling sophomore, will leave a gap in the family for many weeks to come. To whom will I turn for help in solving my problems? Just poor Daddy, the original Great Problem Solver—a trifle worn but still serviceable.

Your baby sister is making a valiant effort to do well at Thayer Academy, but judging by some of her homework papers, she has a long way to go yet. Last night's assignment for English was to write what she thought of the four books she had read this summer. Regarding *Abe Lincoln Grows Up,* she wrote:

"I found this book very hard to get interested in because it was so much like history. (In fact, it *was* history.) There was one good thing about it, though. It made the books I read next seem more interesting by comparison."

Her comment on *Tom Sawyer* was that even though she had seen the movie three times, she liked the book better. She said *Seventeen* was the oddest book she had ever read, but never explained why. *Mutiny on the Bounty* was very exciting and she thought Christian was perfect for the part—whatever that means.

We had a dinner party last Saturday night. During the day we tried to impress on Tim that he shouldn't nag, shouldn't argue, shouldn't complain, shouldn't fight with Vonnie—in other words, he should act as unnatural as possible. He said "Uh-huh, uh-huh," but he couldn't have heard a word we said.

Shortly before our guests were due, I was arranging towels and giving the basin a last hasty polishing when one ear tuned in on something Tim mumbled as he hurried by the doorway. Something about transferring his guppies to Dad's aquarium because the water in the glass bowl smelled bad. When the implications of what I had heard registered on my brain, I dropped everything.

"Timmy!" I yelled, running to the head of the stairs. "*Timmy!* Whatever it was you just said you were going to do, put it off until tomorrow!"

"Don't worry, I won't make any mess" floated faintly back to me. Worried as all get-out, I bellowed, "*Tomorrow,* Timmy!"

I got downstairs just in time to witness the climax to Tim's performance with the goldfish bowl. He had managed to

Growing, growing, gone . . . into darkest adolescence.

transfer the fish with a minimum of splattering over the piano, then had lugged the ill-smelling bowl into the pantry and plunked it into the sink "to wash off the pebbles." Now as he attempted to carry the thing back to his room, it began leaking all over the dining room rug.

"Oops!" he said, wheeling back toward the pantry with the dripping bowl. Plunk, into the sink again, and the doorbell rang as I stood there practically up to my ankles in stagnant water.

"Get the mop," I ordered, grabbing the miserable bowl to put it out of sight. At that moment the bottom fell out and a mass of tiny pebbles went cascading down the drain. "Now look what you've done!" said Tim. Dad stuck his head in the pantry to see what was going on, but all he said was "Good for the plumbing." I left him to help Tim pick up the pieces because *someone* had to put on a big smile and go to the front door.

Not long after this incident Tim called me into the playroom for a private conference. It seemed there was this Ping-Pong ball and it had a little dent in it, so he figured the judicious application of a match would expand the air inside and pop out the dent. Very scientific. Imagine his surprise when the ball exploded into flames. Understandably enough, he dropped it on the floor and stamped on it. He sheepishly pointed out the burn mark while I struggled to keep a straight face. By this time, Timmy's infinite capacity for getting into trouble was striking me as funny.

He has been fairly good today except for swearing at the little girl next door. He didn't swear out loud, he claimed; it was under his breath. "How come your sister heard you, then?" "She must have read my lips."

Lots of love,
Mom

I came down with the flu yesterday and felt so miserable I went to bed for the afternoon. When I wasn't blowing my nose or holding my hands over my ears, I was reading Allen Drury's *Advise and Consent*. What marvelous characterizations, what plot development, what a racket downstairs. I put my hands over my ears again and reminded myself that boys will be boys. Timmy is home on vacation from Moses Brown, as are all his friends; they don't have homes of their own, poor things, so they must release their energy under my sickbed.

All ten boys had to take a turn at playing the piano; since there wasn't a piano player in the lot, this was no Carnegie Hall treat. Then, boys being boys, they got tired of taking turns and all ten of them ganged up on that defenseless piano, pounding it without mercy or letup. The din was so earsplitting that no one could hear me yelling at the top of the stairs. I finally got through with my message, the gist of which was "It's a beautiful day, why don't you little monsters go outside and play?"

They compromised: half of them went outside, the other half stayed in. The ones on the inside filled balloons with water and, from third-floor windows, pelted the ones who were outside. By the time I realized what was going on, the driveway was strewn with tragic little balloon bodies—it looked as if the milkman had run over something. I told Tim to sweep up the mess and he grumbled, "Gee whiz, nobody can have any fun around here."

"Go have fun at somebody else's house for a change," I croaked, and crawled back into bed.

I was hardly settled with my book when the piano came to life again. I didn't think there was a spark left in it, but it's a hardy instrument. Ted was practicing "Too Young." Recently

I made the mistake of teaching Vonnie how to play "Too Young." She compounded the felony by passing her accomplishment on to her brother.

I'll say this for Ted, he doesn't bang the keys. He has a nice gentle touch and he also has all the patience in the world, leaving none for me. The way he practices "Too Young" reminds me of the way my mother writes a poem. She fills page after page with the same six or eight lines until that elusive final stanza finally flows from her pencil. Ted's technique is similar. The first four bars, which he knows cold, must be played over and over and over again until the fifth bar is also perfect, and then on to the sixth.

When Ed got home I announced to him without preamble that if I ever heard him whistle "Too Young" again—on- or off-key—I would get a divorce. It used to be "our song," too.

September 12, 1960
Cohasset

When I saw Ted's campus at Colby this weekend, I was sorry we hadn't brought the movie camera; Lord knows when we'll get up to Maine again. The grounds and buildings were lovely—no big trees as yet in the newly built area, but there's a picturesque pond in the background.

Teddy looked wonderful in his jacket, tie—and *vest* yet! So manly and clean-cut. As we were leaving, he shook hands with his father and gave me a sheepish peck on the cheek. What a contrast, I thought, between this splendid young son and the ruffian I dragged to the police station two years ago for a lecture from Chief Pelletier. Sprawled in a chair in a dirty T-shirt and greasy jeans, clammed up, sullen and uncooperative, he no more resembled the Ted of today than a caterpillar resembles a butterfly. The metamorphosis of an adolescent into an adult is surely one of nature's most gratifying phenomena.

October 5, 1960
Cohasset

Yesterday was my day to pick up the car pool at Thayer. It was Vonnie's day to see if she could drive me out of my mind. A girl named Martha Blanchard was still playing field hockey, so the rest of us had to wait in the car for half an hour. I didn't mind because I had a good book I could read while the young ladies prattled about the shapes, faces, and personalities of their classmates.

Then something distracted me. Vonnie was changing radio stations with her feet. I ordered her to put her shoes back on; that was no way to change the station.

"Why not?" she said, looking injured.

"Because it's lazy and sloppy and it's driving me crazy," I said. There were giggles in the back seat.

The next distraction occurred when I noticed that Vonnie had some strange substance, which she was apparently eating, wrapped around her fingers like Band-Aids.

"Vonnie, what *is* that stuff?"

"Wax," she replied briefly.

"*Wax?* Well, spit it right out and take it off your fingers this minute."

"Why?" said Vonnie, sounding abused.

"*Why?* Because it isn't good for you, that's why. Eating wax! Wrapping it around your fingers! I never heard of anything so silly."

"I'm not eating it, I'm chewing it."

"Chewing *wax?* Vonnie, why do you do these crazy things?"

At this point Martha Blanchard got into the car. I should have smiled and introduced myself, but I was too harassed for social amenities.

"You're *supposed* to chew it," Vonnie said. "It's *fingers*."

This incomprehensible explanation delighted the car pool,

Vonnie included, but no one dared giggle openly. The girls sat, shaking with suppressed laughter, while I drove toward the expressway, feeling very Older Generationish. Finally one of them said something mildly funny, and they all exploded into hysterics.

Eventually the Younger Generation brought the Older Generation up to date on this business of wax fingers and wax lips. It was suggested that these novelties might even have been available during the Halloween season when *I* was a girl—I just didn't remember that far back.

November 14, 1960
Cohasset

Tim wouldn't go to the football game with us last Saturday; he'd rather spend what little time he has at home playing ball with his buddies.

Ed was disappointed but sympathetic, so he, Vonnie, and I drove over to Thayer Academy. On the way she asked me if it was true I had called Emmaline, the proprietor of the record shop, a virgin. I was startled by the question and sure I had never called her any such thing.

"Timmy said you did," Vonnie said.

"Now wait a minute," I said. "If Tim says I did, maybe I did. His memory is better than mine. I wish I knew the circumstances because out of context I don't recognize the remark."

"I still don't think you'd say a thing like that about Emmaline," Vonnie said.

I looked at her suspiciously. "Isn't it nicer for me to say she's a virgin than to say she isn't?"

There was a silence while she thought it over. Finally: "What *is* a virgin, anyway?"

Ed almost lost control of the car.

"You must have *some* idea," I said hopefully.

"I *thought* I did. Isn't it sort of an angel, like Mary? You know, 'Round yon Virgin, mother and child.'"

"*Jesus!*" said Ed.

I tried to explain things, using as an example the illustrious Mary, since I couldn't think of another virgin offhand without getting personal. Suddenly she caught on, gave her father an embarrassed glance, and muttered, "Okay, *okay,* I get it."

Meanwhile I remembered what I said to Tim about Emmaline. I said anyone who was so patient with a bunch of rowdy teenagers, Tim included, was a *saint.*

February 28, 1961
Cohasset

I am in the foulest possible of moods this morning. Right now I wish I had never gone to Betty Allen's birthday party, never met Ed, never gotten married, and, above all, never had children.

Ed feels as I do, only more so. You'd think a man who spends his days grappling with one business crisis after another could at least have the compensation of pride and satisfaction in his family. But what does he come home to? Aggravation.

Ed took one look at Ted's report card, sank into his chair, and said he didn't feel much like attending any more of the loafer's hockey games. Ted got a C minus, three D pluses, and a D minus, which means he is on academic probation.

"But honey," I said, "we can't reject him just because of his marks."

"Don't worry about it," Ted said when his father telephoned him, but how can we help but worry?

As for Tim, his report arrived in yesterday's mail. His only respectable grade was an 88 in mathematics; since his course is a repetition of what he had in Cohasset last year, he should be doing even better. English was 70, Latin 71, biology 60, and deportment "variable."

I dashed off a letter to Tim, then wondered if I had been too harsh and mailed him some cookies. It's so hard to know when you are doing the right thing and when you are blundering. First you think he acts the way he does because you've spoiled him; then you wonder if it's because he feels neglected and unhappy.

When Ed got home he glanced at Timmy's report card and groaned, "I wish I'd never seen it. Can't you hide these things or something?"

I told him I had lectured Tim in a letter, and he sighed that he would do the same.

We were about to go downstairs when the phone rang. It was Mr. Scoble, Vonnie's Spanish teacher. He told me she'd been goofing off. "It's a rare day when she has more than a third of her homework done."

I promised Mr. Scoble I would speak to my daughter.

How *could* she go to class with her homework uncompleted? I still have nightmares in which I find myself unprepared in class. How did I beget such a giddy, empty-headed little goose? What will *become* of her?

And what will become of that other affliction, her younger brother? Timmy called from Moses Brown this morning and said in an abused voice that he was in trouble again.

"Good grief, what *now!*"

There was a fifteen-cent pause during which he tried to figure out why the old lady was getting so upset *already*.

"It's Mr. Bradley again," he said finally. The artful use of the word "again" implied that the reckless Mr. Bradley is always at the bottom of these things. "He asked me to do something unreasonable and I refused to do it."

"You mean you defied him?" I moaned. "*Why?*"

"Because what he asked was unreasonable," Tim repeated sulkily.

"Timmy, you just can't go around challenging authority

like that. It may have seemed unreasonable to you, but I'm sure it was perfectly reasonable to Mr. Bradley."

"If I told you what it was, you wouldn't think it was reasonable either," he said with a conviction that gave me pause. Why was he being so mysterious? Surely this Mr. Bradley wasn't some sort of degenerate.

"Why don't you tell me what happened from the beginning," I said, bracing myself for God knew what.

"Well, these other kids and I were coming down the stairs and Mr. Bradley comes out of his room real mad and wants to know who's making all the noise. Nobody says anything, so then he wants to know who was the last one down the stairs and this kid points at me. I wasn't making any more noise than anyone else, but Mr. Bradley tells me to come into his apartment, he wants to talk to me."

"Good heavens," I thought.

"Then he tells me to take off my shoes—"

"Take off your *shoes?*"

"I told you he was unreasonable. He said to take off my shoes and come back for them at the end of the week. They were the only shoes I had, so I told him I wouldn't do it."

"Then for God's sake go out and buy yourself another pair. Go back to Mr. Bradley and apologize and straighten this mess out, or we'll send you to a school where you'll have more to worry about than taking your shoes off."

I made a few more choice threats and banged down the receiver. After I stopped quivering I dialed the office and bleated the latest tidings to Ed.

"Hadn't you better call the school and find out what's happening?"

"I'll think about it while I have my coffee," he said. "Let him stew for a while, it'll do him good."

Ed called back and said he'd just had a long talk with the

headmaster. "As I understand it, here's what happened. Tim and a couple of other kids are coming down the stairs and they decide to skip the last two or three steps. The three clowns jump simultaneously and land with a crash outside a classroom. Mr. Bradley comes storming out, and when he sees Timmy he blows his top. It isn't just this one thing, you see, it's one thing after another."

Mr. Whittier told Ed that Tim's misbehavior is never so serious that they can make a federal case of it. For instance, they learned he's been keeping a cigarette lighter in his room. He says he's not smoking and they believe him, but they're nervous about this lighter. The dormitories are old wooden buildings that could easily go up in flames.

Tim gives them a spirited argument. He says, you know I'm not smoking, why can't I keep a cigarette lighter in my room, is there a rule against having a cigarette lighter? Mr. Whittier admits there is no such rule, because until Tim came along, it didn't seem necessary.

Other new rules inspired by our son: No Throwing Snowballs at Cars from Your Dormitory Window and No Keeping a Slingshot in Your Room with Which to Snipe at Squirrels.

I try, really I do. When we came home from Florida with those firecrackers I thought I'd forestall trouble at Moses Brown by establishing the rule No Bringing Firecrackers to School. Tim said scornfully, "Don't be silly, do you think I want to get kicked out?"

"He has these poor people in a tizzy all the time," Ed concluded. "They're going to give him another chance, but one more misstep and out he goes."

I went down to the kitchen to make myself a sandwich. My head felt as if it were full of hornets. To round out the day, Tokay, whom I had taken for a number of walks without result, finally performed on the living room rug and hid under a chair; the cat's ear infection flared up again and I had to take her to the vet; and Ed called to say he wouldn't be home until late, he was going to Worcester.

While I was having dinner in the kitchen I heard Kathryn filling Vaughan in on what had taken place on *Young Dr. Malone.* It seemed that Claire was in a coma. Dr. Malone had delivered her baby but it was born dead. Vaughan asked what was going to become of the property and Kathryn said she didn't know, it all depended on who was the father of the baby.

I was glad to hear about Claire's problems; mine seemed so trivial by comparison.

March 4, 1961
Cohasset

Vonnie's driving technique has improved considerably with a week of constant practice, and yesterday she passed her test with little difficulty. When the inspector handed her her temporary license and got out of the car, she collapsed on the wheel as if she had been stabbed. Then she hugged me and half cried with relief.

Now she was a pro. On the way back to Thayer I was not permitted to make the most minor suggestion about her driving. "I have my license," she growled in the guttural voice she has been cultivating of late, two octaves below basso profundo.

"People, I have my license," she growled out the window at staring pedestrians.

I kept looking at her, remembering the small bundle the nurse put into my arms some sixteen years ago—the tiny head dusted with flaxen down, the china-doll face, the delicate complexion . . .

Vonnie got back to school in time for lunch.

"The funniest thing happened in the lunchroom," she told me later. "I was so excited about getting my license I kept banging Gloria on the back with my pocketbook and all of a sudden smoke started to pour out of it. I had a packet of matches in there and I guess they caught fire by friction or something."

"Oh, no," I said weakly.

"And I had my license in there—"

"Oh, no!" I shut my eyes.

"—and three firecrackers."

"*No!*" I was spellbound.

"I threw it on the floor and jumped up and down on it until it stopped smoking. Wasn't it lucky the firecrackers didn't go off?"

"It was lucky indeed," I said, "since you probably would have been expelled. May I ask why you had three firecrackers in your purse?"

"I was going to set them off down on the beach to celebrate getting my license."

Why, naturally.

June 24, 1962
Cohasset

Kathryn left yesterday. She seemed surprised that I wasn't angry with her and said to Mother, "In her place I'd feel like kicking me in the pants."

I admit I was shocked when she first broke the news about her job in Maine ("I don't know whether this is going to be good news or bad, Mrs. Malley," she began modestly). But thinking it over, I realized she had a right to think of herself and her approaching old age. She is sixty-one years old and may not have many working years ahead of her. Of course we would have looked out for her, if her children didn't, just as we had for Vaughan, but I can't blame her for wanting to be independent. As a pastry cook she will be getting seventy-five dollars a week, almost double what I pay her, and her Social Security benefits will be that much higher.

Before she left, Kathryn made an apple pie to end all apple pies—one of her huge rectangular affairs, loaded with plump spicy apples, covered with the tenderest of crusts, and filling the house with a heavenly aroma. Mother asked her at least five times if the pie was ready yet. Even I broke down and poured cream over a square while it was still hot.

"Kathryn, this is the best apple pie you've ever made," I said. "Why are you torturing us like this?"

It took her a day to pack. Kathie and Ted helped her lug out carton after carton of belongings accumulated during her years with us. Although I had invited her to store anything she wanted to in the barn, she managed to cram the lot into her car.

"Someday my grandchildren can pick over all this stuff, take what they want, and then as far as I'm concerned they can burn the rest. Don't ever move, Mrs. Malley."

I kissed her good-bye and wished her luck but said I hoped she'd *hate* her new job and come running back to the Malleys.

Meanwhile, if I don't find someone else I'm going to try to manage by myself. There will be seven of us, but Vonnie has agreed to help for a price, Kathie for love, and Mom, too, enjoys making herself useful. Vaughan's move to the nursing home has eased the pressure here, and I think she is contented.

September 27, 1962
Cohasset

I had my lunch at noon and fed the kittens. They were still busily pushing their dishes around when I went upstairs, so I was surprised to hear a mewing sound in Vonnie's room.

"Here, kitty," I called, wondering how the rascal had beaten me up the stairs. "Here, kitty."

I looked under the beds. No kitty. There was another piercing mew. I turned my head toward Vonnie's desk, and out toddled the black-and-white kitten. But what had happened to it? It had *shrunk*. Yes, it definitely had shrunk; it looked tinier than it did a month ago. Was I having hallucinations or—

"*Vonnie!*"

I picked up the squirming bit of fluff and marched downstairs to talk to my daughter. As everyone knows, Daddy discusses these things quietly and reasonably. Mummy blows her top. Today was no exception.

"Y-e-e-s, Mummy?" Vonnie asked guiltily.

"Just what is *this,* may I ask?"

"It's a kitten."

"I know it's a kitten," I said crossly. "Where did you get it?"

"Karen left it with me."

"Stephanie Vaughan Malley, what on earth are you thinking of? We already have two kittens—two female kittens, at that—and a pregnant poodle. What kind of zoo do you think we're running here? You tell Karen we've got all the animals we want and give this—this—*thing* back to her!" By now I was too mad to call it as cute a name as "kitten."

"But the McKennas have gone back to Boston. Don't worry, I'm not keeping it, Mummy. I'm going to find a home for it as soon as it's big enough."

"That's the McKennas' problem, not ours."

"I'm doing it as a favor for Karen. She asked me to take care of them until—"

"*Them?* What do you mean, *them?*"

"There's three of them," Vonnie said, drawing a line on the rug with her toe.

At this, there was a whoop from my new housekeeper, Mrs. Wright, who had been quietly snickering as she dusted the dining room table.

"Three of them?" I moaned. "For Pete's sake, *where?*"

"In a box under my desk."

Mrs. Wright was now giggling quite openly. I pointed a stern finger at this traitor to all that was sane and sensible in the world of adults. "*You* be quiet," I ordered.

She clapped her hand over her mouth and tried to look solemn, but the more I ranted at Vonnie, the more she lost control. She finally had to retire to the kitchen to pull herself together.

I have called the Animal Rescue League. The truck is coming on Friday. If Vonnie can find homes for them in the meantime, fine—otherwise, out they go, no matter how sweet and little and appealing they are. One has to draw the line *somewhere*.

October 5, 1962
Cohasset

Things have never been quieter at Malley's Madhouse. If we don't have a little action, reaction, and interaction around here, I'll begin to think I'm dreaming. Vonnie is being an angel, and David Timothy is becoming more Davidish and less Timmyish every day.

With life progressing so peacefully, Vonnie and I are having trouble finding anything to say to our psychiatrists, whom the school suggested we see about her high spirits and teenage rebelliousness. I've told Dr. Altman all I can remember of youthful traumatic experiences, and I have admitted that at Vonnie's age I was a silly, boy-crazy girl. But what difference does *that* make? I've grown up. I'm a mature, man-crazy woman.

Vonnie said yesterday, "I almost wish something would go wrong, so I'd have something to talk about with Dr. Chan."

"Why don't you tell her what you just told me, about stay-ing after school for your science teacher?"

"Oh, she wouldn't want to hear anything like that. She'd just sit there and smile her little smile and when I finished, she'd say, 'Oh, really?' or 'Is that so?'"

Vonnie had received her first detention this semester be-cause she laughed at something Joanne Patterson said as the teacher was bringing the class to order. When she presented herself after class, he asked her if she knew why she was there.

"I said I didn't, but of course I really did. Then he asked me to write an essay on the subject of talking. I looked up the word 'talk' in the dictionary and wrote an essay describing the difference between talking and laughing. I ended by say-ing, 'And so, my dear professor, even though I have been un-justly accused, I forgive you because the sentence is the same in either case.'"

I asked her what had made her laugh.

"You'll kill me if I tell you." I promised not to kill her, so she said, "Joanne has a charm bracelet, and one of the charms is a pair of dice. We were shooting craps."

October 20, 1962
Cohasset

Tim painted his car blue the other day, using as a paint bucket the new plastic pail I had just bought for Mrs. Wright. First time I've seen her annoyed with him.

The next day he told me Stevie Hodgkins was coming over to paint *his* car.

"Why doesn't he paint his car at his own house?"

"Because he doesn't have a good place to do it."

Or because his mother knows him better than I do. Put a paint sprayer in the kid's hand and he goes beserk. When I got home from Boston that afternoon, there was Stevie's car, a gleaming, screaming, ax-murder red. And there was our garage, looking like the scene of the crime. It was as if Stevie had plenty of paint left and hated to waste it. A red film had been sprayed on floor, walls, workbench, lawn mower, garden tools, and Gail Emerson's bicycle. The effect was heart-stopping. Oh, Stevie Hodgkins, what have you done!

I asked him that question over the telephone. He was apologetic. It was getting dark when he finished, he said, and he hadn't realized . . . he thought maybe he had accidentally sprayed a little red paint on top of Timmy's blue paint, but he hadn't meant . . . well, he was awfully sorry, and he'd gladly make good on it.

The only remedy I can think of is to set a match to the place and start over. Or call it Malley's Paint and Body Shop and go into business.

November 2, 1963
Fort Lauderdale, Florida

Last night I read Amy Vanderbilt's column in *McCall's* and learned she has some suggestions for coping with noisy family dinners. A woman had written complaining that she was constantly shushing her children and was a nervous wreck by the end of meals served in the kitchen. She was afraid to let them loose in the dining room except on rare occasions when there were special guests. Her two boys "and a very noisy girl" were giving her indigestion. Did the columnist have any ideas?

Miss Vanderbilt's answer: "First, before you blame the children, try the dining room with just the family. Three children at any table usually create a certain amount of noise just through conversation, and it may be your kitchen that is at fault. It may have surfaces that throw back the sound. . . . Try putting baffles in your kitchen—cushions on the chairs, a rug at the dining end, window curtains made of burlap or hopsacking. Lower your own tone of voice in speaking to the children and ask your husband to do the same. Children learn table manners through precept and example."

I feel so ashamed. All these years I'd been blaming our noisy dinners on Timmy, but now I realize it was the kitchen's fault. If only I'd had the benefit of Miss Vanderbilt's advice years ago, how different things might have been.

Time: November 1955.
Place: The Malley family's dining room. It is 6:00 p.m. The table is set for dinner. One window to the left of stage and a pair of French doors to the right are concealed under yards of burlap. Also wrapped in burlap are the chandelier over the table and the buffet, rear center. Clearly, someone in the house has a flair for the daring and original in interior decorating. Six chairs are drawn up to the table; on each is a cushion borrowed from the living room sofa. If the dining room could speak, it would say "I'm thoroughly baffled."
[Enter, through swinging door on left, MOTHER. *She, too, looks baffled.]*
MOTHER. My, but it's dark in here! Oh, I forgot to light the candles. Ed, are there any matches around?
[Enter, from hallway, right of stage, FATHER.*]*
FATHER. What's the matter, did you blow a fuse?
MOTHER. No, silly, we're having dinner by candlelight. Ask Timmy if he has any matches.
FATHER. Timmy! *Timmy!* DAVID TIMOTHY MALLEY!
MOTHER. Dear, we must remember to keep our voices low so the children will learn from our precept and example.
VOICE FROM HALL. Did someone call me?
[Enter TIMMY, *a precocious nine-year-old. He has not yet taken up smoking but can usually be counted on to have*

matches in his pocket. He is eating a Mars Bar and reading Mad *magazine.* FATHER *and* MOTHER *speak in unison.]*

FATHER. Timmy, you'll ruin your eyes.

MOTHER. Timmy, you'll ruin your dinner.

[Continuing to eat candy bar and read magazine two inches from his face, TIMMY *stumbles over* FATHER'S *foot and sprawls on floor.]*

TIMMY [*accusingly*]. You tripped me!

FATHER [*indignantly*]. I did not trip you!

TIMMY. You did, too!

FATHER. I did not!

MOTHER. Boys, *please.* We're going to keep our voices low tonight, remember?

TIMMY [*more quietly*]. You did, too. Hey, Maw, why don't you put the lights on?

MOTHER. They *are* on, dear.

TIMMY. What's that potato sack doing on the chandelier?

FATHER. That's a good question.

MOTHER. I got the idea from a magazine. I don't have time to explain it now. Timmy, do you have a match so I can light the candles?

TIMMY [*producing packet of matches*]. I want to light the candles.

[Enter, from hall, eleven-year-old VONNIE, *a Very Noisy Girl.]*

VONNIE [*raucously*]. I want to light the candles!

TIMMY [*yelling*]. I'm going to light the candles!

MOTHER [*blocking ears and looking reproachfully at burlap-covered chandelier*]. It threw the sound right back at me.

VONNIE [*shouting*]. Why should you light the candles? You lit them the last time!

MOTHER [*firmly*]. I'll light the candles.

TIMMY [*holding matches behind his back*]. They're my matches.

[FATHER *and* MOTHER *look at each other.*]

FATHER. He has a point there.

MOTHER. All right, Timmy, you may light the candles.

VONNIE [*tearfully*]. Why does he always have to get his way?

MOTHER. Don't suck your thumb, dear. I'll tell you what, you can blow them out—would that make you happy?

VONNIE. Oh, boy!

[*She blows out candles and room is shrouded in darkness.*]

MOTHER. I meant after dinner, Vonnie.

[TIMMY *relights candles.*]

VONNIE [*pouting*]. Timmy got to light the candles twice. When it's my turn, I want to light them twice, too.

[*Enter thirteen-year-old* TEDDY, *an all-American boy with a diversity of hobbies and interests. He is riding a motorcycle, wearing his football uniform, and carrying a .22 rifle in one hand and a copy of* Dude *magazine in the other. A cracker-jack marksman, he recently succeeded, at two hundred paces and with one hand tied behind him, in breaking every pane of glass in Mr. McKenna's barn.*]

FATHER. Teddy, you know you're not supposed to ride that thing in the dining room.

MOTHER. Yes, Ted, put your toys away now, it's time for dinner.

TEDDY [*slinging the rifle over his shoulder*]. I won't shoot it at the table, honest, Mom.

MOTHER. Well, all right, but remember—you promised.

FATHER [*sternly*]. I'll take that magazine, Ted.

TEDDY [*reluctantly handing magazine to* FATHER]. Awww, why don'tcha buy your own?

MOTHER [*going to hallway and calling upstairs*]. Kathie, dinner's ready.

FATHER [*eyes bulging as he studies an artistic representation in* Dude *magazine*]. Wow!

MOTHER [*sternly*]. I'll take that magazine, Ed.

FATHER. Awww.

[Enter the oldest child in the family, a moody fifteen-year-old girl. Her noisy brothers and her very noisy sister don't see much of KATHIE, *since she is usually locked in her room. This is not a disciplinary measure but a self-imposed exile. She doesn't like noise. In fact, she finds her family in general almost more than she can bear. Engrossed in a book called* Horses Are the Best People, *by Ima Morgan, she bumps into Teddy's motorcycle. It crashes resoundingly to the floor.]*

KATHIE *[heatedly].* Teddy, must you bring that stupid contraption into the dining room?

TEDDY *[mildly].* What do you expect me to do—walk?

KATHIE. Someday I'm going to ride my horse in here. If you can keep your motorcycle in the house, why should Heidi have to stay out in the barn?

[All members of the family speak simultaneously.]

TEDDY *[considering the matter].* Well, for one thing, my motorcycle is housebroken.

VONNIE *[eagerly].* Will you let me ride double, Kathie?

MOTHER *[nervously].* I'd rather you didn't, dear.

FATHER *[pacifically].* Now, Sunshine . . .

TIMMY.

[Writer is interrupted by real-life husband and brought abruptly back to the present.]

I've got to stop here. Ed's threatening to go to the beach without me and ogle all the pretty girls.

What does Timmy say? And what does Mother finally do? I suspect in the end she fires off a letter to *McCall's* magazine.

"Dear Amy: Having followed your advice, may I suggest a burlap bag for your head? Signed, Distraught Mother of Four Noisy Children."

January 4, 1964
Cohasset

I've just finished reading Richard Armour's *Through Dark-est Adolescence*. Aside from being very funny, it is a comforting book. We are not singular, Ed and I. There are others like us, confused, miserable, and downtrodden, driven beserk by the incomprehensible behavior of their teenagers. Would that we could be as successful as Mr. Armour in clinging to our senses of humor. I am going to order half a dozen copies to give to friends in the same boat as we are—they might as well enjoy a chuckle as the ship goes down.

September 16, 1965
Cohasset

The time, 5:00 A.M. The occasion, The Day Timmy Went to College. Let's wave a few banners, blow a few trumpets, say a few prayers. The last fledgling has left the nest.

He shook hands with his father and said, "Have a little faith for a change, will you, Dad?"

"That's just what I have," Ed said. "A little faith. The first year will be the toughest. If you can get through that, it'll be duck soup."

"I don't think I'll have too much trouble—my schedule's pretty easy. The main thing I want to figure out is what I want to be and do. Rich and nothing," he decided, giving us a wave and starting down the stairs.

"Good-bye, Tim."

"Good-bye, Mom. Good-bye, Dad."

Ed and I returned to our beds, well pleased with our agreeable, nonargumentative parting with our son.

"Just think!" I marveled. "For the first time in twenty-five years I'm free. Absolutely free."

"No, you're not," Ed said. "We're never free."

"That's the way I feel," I insisted, closing my eyes and wrapping my arms around my pillow. "Free as a bird. No responsibilities, no worries—"

CLONK . . . CLONK . . . CLONK . . . CLONK . . .

The noise sounded as if someone were trying to demolish *Old Ironsides* with a sledgehammer.

"Good grief, what on earth is he doing?"

More *clonk*'s, louder.

"He's going to wake the whole neighborhood!" I jumped out of bed, ran down the stairs, flung open the front door.

"Timmy, what *are* you doing?"

"Trying to close the trunk of my car."

"Well, don't do it *here,* for heaven's sake. Don't you realize people are trying to sleep?"

Without saying anything, he climbed into his car and started it up. Regretful that I had spoken to him so sharply, I called after him, "Good-bye, Tim!"

I went back to bed and reported to Ed that our boy was on his way at last.

"Well, you've got him as far as the end of the driveway, anyway."

CLONK . . . CLONK . . . CLONK . . .

He called a few minutes ago to say he needs blankets, a pillow, Leslie's shoes are in his car, and he misses her already.

Four

Of Unexpected Pregnancies and Reluctant Grandfathers (1964–1965/1939–1947)

September 4, 1964
Cohasset, Massachusetts

Vonnie has an excellent reason for refusing to return to junior college. She's pregnant.

While her letter is no bombshell, it doesn't make us feel like opening champagne. We're worried sick about her future—or at least I am. Ed says she's out of his life now; he's not going to tear himself apart, he has enough problems.

But how can she be happy once she discovers that marriage and courtship are not synonymous? I can't picture her learning to scrimp, economize, do without, in order to live on a mailman's salary. She insists she loves Bob and wants to marry him. "You can disown me," she said in her letter, "or you can give us your blessings and wish us luck." Ed leans toward disowning.

In her unmethodical way, she is vague about the date of our first grandchild's arrival. "Well, how late are you?" "Oh, I don't know, a month or two, I guess."

Kathie and her daddy, 1941.

How can this child be responsible for a child?
And yet . . . she's a year older than I was. . . .

December 10, 1939
Smith College
Northampton, Massachusetts

Though I'm only a couple of days late, I'm so sure I'm caught
I can't think of anything else for more than five minutes. God,
what a fool I am. Why didn't I keep my resolve to see Eddie
only on a platonic basis? And if I had to give in, why was I so

careless? I can't blame him. *I* was the one who got carried away. The entire course of my life could be changed by a few reckless moments.

Having to leave college after only one semester will be bad enough. But what will I tell the trusting people who gave me a scholarship? And Mr. Rinker, with his faith in my future as a writer? And Mother! How will I face Mother?

If I'm pregnant, I see only one choice: I'll have to convince everyone, Eddie included—*myself* included—that I don't mind leaving college to get married.

December 12, 1939
Smith College
Northampton

To Eddie Malley

How did you feel when you woke up this morning? Full of high spirits, I am sure—raring to go (jump off a cliff, no doubt).

It seems kind of pointless to work on my source theme now. For my part, I find it hard to work on anything—even to write letters. What I'd like to do would be to crawl into bed, pull the covers over my head, and *hibernate* for the next *nine* months. And I don't want to see anybody until I come out.

December 14, 1939
Boston

From Eddie

Without the confirmation of a medical expert, I hesitate to say that I fear you are slightly demented. Don't start worrying yet; it probably isn't serious. You certainly aren't violent or dangerous—I hope. I promise you that I shall always take into consideration your irrational condition and treat you accordingly. With a strong and firm hand, I'll lead you along life's stony path and protect you from the world's inhabitants who, though they are not as mad as you, are probably not as happy. There, my little lunatic, does that make you feel better?

As for myself, I almost hope that "worse comes to worst" and my life will become part of yours for always. Please do not feel that I blame you for making my life a "mess" or for depriving me of my "liberty." It is only with you that I could ever be truly contented.

December 16, 1939
Smith College
Northampton

I still can't believe I'm pregnant. It can't be *that* easy to have a baby. Every ten minutes I go to the lavatory and look desperately for a tinge of pink. Pink that will deepen to red. Red for redemption. My dormmates must think I have the runs.

December 17, 1939
Boston

From Eddie

Dear Babs,
   1. I love you.
   2. I hope you have our baby.
   3. *You love me.* (I hope)
   4. You must believe in me.
   5. It's 2 A.M. and I'm tired.
   6. My business deal is progressing.
   7. Merry Christmas and a Happy New Year.

8. Think of me once in a while.

9. All of my love is for you, darling. Forever and always.

Twenty-five years later, my first reaction to Vonnie's pregnancy was less than empathetic. A phone call revised my perspective.

September 8, 1964
Cohasset

Forty-eight hours ago I wouldn't have believed I could have such a change of heart. I got up this morning feeling more discouraged than ever about Vonnie. Then Bob's mother called. She said the kids had just told her they were getting married and of course it was a shock, Bob is her only son, and she knew how disappointed we must feel, too. It wasn't a very good way to start out, but after all, what was done was done. After the wedding, she and her husband were going to have a little reception so all Bob's relatives—"and we have a flock of them!"—could meet the bride.

"If you and your husband would care to join us, we'd love to have you—and anyone else who might like to come would be most welcome. Our doors are always open."

This warmhearted person changed my point of view completely. I knew changing Ed's would be a tall order, however.

"Now, honey, before you fly off the handle and say no, will you listen to me for a minute? I just had a nice long talk with Mrs. Crosby and—"

"*Who?*"

"Mrs. Crosby. *Bob's* mother. You know, Vonnie's prospective—"

"Oh. What did *she* want?" (Growl.)

"Well, she sounds like a very nice person. She and her husband were disappointed just the way we were, but she says what's done is done, so after the wedding they're having a reception and they want us to—"

"*No!* I won't go! I positively won't do it!"

He didn't hang up, though, so I kept talking and he said, "Boy, have *you* changed. What's come over *you* all of a sudden?"

"It's Bob's mother. Don't you see how *right* she is? Sure, maybe all our gloomy predictions will come true, maybe they'll be fed up with marriage inside of a week, but it isn't going to help them if we turn our backs on them."

"Okay, okay," he finally said in his I'll-never-understand-women tone of voice. "I'll go. For your sake. Why should I make things any tougher for you than they've been already."

Smith College policy in 1939, like that of most women's colleges, was to eject any pregnant student at the end of the current semester, and married women were not allowed to enroll. Determined to continue my education, I looked desperately for alternatives and loopholes.

December 20, 1939
Newton Center, Massachusetts

I see no way out of my dilemma except to marry Eddie, then divorce him as soon as possible after the baby is born. Only then will I be in a position to resume my college career. If I were accepted at Wellesley or Northeastern, I could live at home and help with the baby's care. Eddie could visit us, and we might even start dating again.

Eddie is all for getting married, but he hopes I'll change my mind about the divorce. "Why would you need college? I'll take care of you," he promises.

When I met Ed I told him I'd always wanted four children, but I fully intended to finish college first. He doesn't understand my yearning to fulfill this dream.

January 1, 1940
Boston

I am now Mrs. Edward Malley. We were married in New Hampshire by a justice of the peace. As he was about to knock on the door, Eddie turned to me and said, "Are you sure you want to go through with this?" (Egad, what a question!)

My wedding finery consisted of a plaid skirt and jacket, scuffed saddle shoes and ankle socks (one with a hole in the heel).

September 10, 1964
Cohasset

It was a busy day. Vonnie asked if her little light gray suit and my white blouse would be appropriate, and I said I thought it would be just right. Mother decided to wear her teal blue suit and a flowered hat. I chose my green wool, the one Ed doesn't like but everybody else does. We took turns using the iron. Vonnie set her hair three different times and still wasn't satisfied. "Why can't it look the way it did *yesterday?*"

She came down to the kitchen with a sheaf of papers under her arm. "My drawings," she said, spreading them out for her grandmother and me to admire one last time. "There won't be room for them in the cottage. Where shall I put them?"

"How about one of the cupboards on the third floor?"

"All right," she said, gathering up her sketches. Then she added wistfully, "Will you go up and look at them once in a while?"

The justice of the peace, Mr. Christianson, performed a brief but beautiful ceremony. Weddings are always beautiful if you really listen to the words.

At 8:00 P.M the "clan" began assembling at the Crosbys' house. Ed and I were stunned to see what had been accomplished on such short notice. Aunts and cousins, contributing platters of lobster rolls, sandwiches, and homemade cookies, had decorated the table and placed a three-tiered wedding cake (made by Aunt Gert) in the middle. All of Bob's relatives were delightful, outgoing, down-to-earth people; I was happy we hadn't missed the event, despite all the misgivings.

When we made our farewells, Ed kissed Vonnie (to whom he had barely spoken for the last week) and shook hands with Bob.

April 29, 1940
Boston

Yesterday Mother and I went over to the Andersens' to see Taffy's new niece. I wandered into the dining room, where my eye fell on something unusual on the table. It was Dot's baby, lying in a basket, surrounded by presents. I still didn't catch on.

Then I saw the other people in the room—it was a baby shower. Never was a surprise party a more successful surprise. When I realized that this had all been done for me, I flung my arms around Taffy and could hardly keep from crying. Many of the guests were girls I hadn't seen since the end of high school, but Taffy said they all jumped at the chance to come.

After I opened the gifts, most of them thoughtfully pink for that girl baby I want so much, Taffy handed me a package. "From your best beau," she said.

"That's Eddie, but he's in New Hampshire," I said, tearing the wrappings from three long-stemmed red roses, "— isn't he?"

"He's here."

I found him upstairs, sunburned after his weekend in the country. "I couldn't stand being away from you any longer," he said. "I *had* to come back this afternoon."

Then he told me he would never let me go without a fight, that he would rather live with me hating him than live apart.

I said I had grown to care for him more than I had believed possible, but felt I owed myself the chance to get my degree. Perhaps someday, if neither of us marries, we might start dating again.

"We'll see what the future brings," Eddie said.

March 18, 1965
Cohasset

Bob's Aunt Gert had a shower for Vonnie a few nights ago. There was some talk about forewarning her "because she's so excitable she might have the baby then and there," but the hazard was risked. Our unexpectant expectant mother breezed in at 8:00, under the impression that she was going to see an evening of home movies. When she saw the festooned table, the gifts, and the beaming faces in the living room, she exclaimed, "Did *he* know?" at Bob's retreating back. He made his escape.

Vonnie looked beautiful. She was wearing a bright red two-piece maternity dress, and her hair was less teased than usual, just softly brushed and turned up at the ends. She looked like someone's red-and-gold valentine with "Guess who?" inside.

Vonnie had found the dress at the Bargain Center, marked

down to a dollar. Our once extravagant daughter is now a bargain hunter. "Once in a while Bob gives me an extra five dollars and tells me to buy myself something," she said the other day. "I just can't do it, Mummy. I either put it in the bank or I go out and buy something for the kitchen."

The baby clothes were all in blue, yellow, or white. Nothing pink. I'll have fun buying dresses if my grandson turns out to be a granddaughter.

August 29, 1940
Boston Lying-in Hospital

I was awake, having strong labor pains, when they wheeled me into the delivery room. Oh, that blessed ether! It hardly seemed a minute later that a voice said, "Look at your little girl, Mrs. Malley."

A *girl*. Born at 6:30 A.M., August 28.

I don't recognize the baby at all. I can't think of it yet as having any sex or being part of me. It's just an "it," a stubborn little "it" that does nothing but sleep and won't eat its dinner. I was upset about this until a nurse told me babies sometimes don't suckle until the second or third day.

August 30, 1940
Boston Lying-in Hospital

I'm so happy I could cry—in fact, I did cry. Kathie finally ate her breakfast this morning, but my, was she stubborn about it. The nurse was so mean to her I could hardly stand it. She pinched and prodded the poor infant and made her wail so pathetically that I was about to say, "*Please* leave her alone," when suddenly she began to nurse. What ecstasy! It seemed as if I could see her filling out under my very eyes.

March 25, 1965
Cohasset

Gazing through the nursery window at Michael Wayne Crosby, I murmured to Ed, "Isn't he beautiful?"

"Humph! I've had a million of 'em," he said.

"Don't exaggerate, dear, it just *seems* like a million."

Vonnie's report after Michael's first feeding: "He's a little pig. He finished his bottle in ten minutes flat. They leave the babies with you for an hour, so I had all that time to play with him. He could only get one eye open. It was dark blue. At the end of the hour he managed to get the other eye open. It was dark blue, too."

I asked Vonnie if she was going to have the baby circumcised and learned she didn't know what the word meant. After I enlightened her, I suggested she talk the matter over with Bob and her doctor. The next time I saw her she said, "I've decided I'm going to go ahead and have the baby . . . castra—— . . . what was that word, Mummy?"

"Good grief!" I said, unmanned at the very thought. *"Circumcised*, Vonnie. Make sure the doctor has it straight."

With that little misunderstanding cleared up, Vonnie told me she was introduced to another new word when the nurse brought a bedpan.

"Did you void?" asked the nurse, returning a few minutes later.

"No," Vonnie said bashfully, "but I urinated."

"That's what I meant," the nurse said, staggering out to the corridor, where she repeated the conversation to hilarious co-workers.

Vonnie told me this story amid fits of giggles alternated with gasps of pain. "I've had to learn an entire new way to laugh, Mummy. I used to laugh with my whole body, but if I did that now my stitches would be right over in that corner. If

I just let the surface of my stomach joggle a bit when I feel a chuckle coming on, it doesn't hurt so much."

She said she cries often, too, but her tears are tears of happiness. "I lie here thinking of how lucky Bob and I are. We had so much before and now we have this darling little baby to love."

Eddie and I lived together in a tiny Boston apartment until Kathie was born. When she was two months old, I took her to Florida and moved in with my mother, who was, with difficulty, supporting herself by taking in roomers in a small rented house in Coral Gables. I enrolled in shorthand, typing, accounting, and Spanish courses at the Walsh School of Business Science in November. Florida in those days was noted for quickie divorces. I filed for divorce (twenty-five dollars down plus fifty dollars later) in November and secured an interim decree. The divorce would become final, without my even having to appear in court, after ninety days.

But Eddie was not a man to let his ardor be cooled or his will thwarted by a mere divorce decree. He continued his courtship by mail.

October 27, 1940
Coral Gables, Florida
To Eddie

Dear Eddie,

It's a good thing you got us the Pullman seat to New York. Kathie and I were comfortable and our fellow passengers were *so* friendly and interested in the baby. Kathie got more attention than a movie star. One woman, however, looked ready to report me as an unfit mother when I changed her clothes right there in public.

Baby and I both stood the strain of the journey pretty well; but I had to stand in line for almost half an hour when we actually arrived in Miami, holding her while the passengers in front of us were getting off. Kathie began to sweat and cried her head off. I was ready to scream. At last I found myself in the automobile with Mother and my wailing baby. The crying upset Mother so much that she drove more erratically than ever. When I was finally left alone with the baby, I broke down and cried.

And now, my poor sweet husband, I feel guilty because I am having such a wonderful time. All the houses in Coral Gables are adobe style—the most colorful, adorable little places you can imagine. Oh, Eddie, you would love it here! You should see the beautiful island homes, with big yachts anchored right by the front door.

Mary, mother's maid, is just wonderful. Last night we had real Southern fried chicken with crispy, crumby skin. She's so helpful and obliging. She does all the baby's laundry for me.

We went to the beach today. The water was divine and I am already quite bronzed. Oh, Eddie, I *do* wish you were here to enjoy all this with me. I hate myself for being happy when you aren't.

About "us," my darling, I *still* don't know.

October 31, 1940
2:00 a.m.
Boston

From Eddie

Dear, dear Mrs. Malley,
Damn Coral Gables, damn the nice weather, damn the silver sands. Damn everything that keeps me from you.

I shall haunt you all the days of our lives. *My* love is a fire that shall burn unquenchable in *your* heart. Though a dozen other men marry you, though you are a million miles away, I shall not yield you—you are mine!

It is really wonderful to love someone. . . .

Thursday
November 14, 1940
11:30 p.m.
Boston

From Eddie

Dearest dear,

I want to come to Florida. Maybe I'm foolish to expose myself to further heartbreak but I'll have to take that chance as I want to see Kathie. I see from her pictures that she is getting *big*. She is going to be a veritable Queen of the Amazons.

Questions:

Why didn't you write Saturday night? (I'm suspicious.)

Why can't you want me more than all those other silly things?

Why don't you start arming yourself *now* against my charm?

Why must time pass so slowly?

Do you miss me?

Why do I love a funny-face like you?

If I mean anything to you, please let me come to you once again. The prospect of seeing you is the only thing that keeps me going.

Saturday night
November 16, 1940
Coral Gables
To Eddie

Dear Eddie—

If you come down at Christmas, I can imagine what will happen. You will sweep me off my hinges. You'll have a lot of money saved up; you'll give me a gay whirl; I'll remember how lonely I was away from you—and how will I be able to resist you?

Eddie's Christmas letter was winning.

Monday
December 23, 1940
Boston
From Eddie

Barbara dearest,

Do you know what you and I are going to do tonight? Well, we're going to set up our first Christmas tree. I've been to the five-and-ten and purchased tinsel, garlands, and ornaments. Isn't the tree a beauty? Where shall we put it?

Now, Barbara, I know Kathie is curious but she must not crawl in the way of her very busy daddy. If we don't do this just right, Santa might miss our chimney. You too must be good or you won't get any presents.

Why don't you make some popcorn for stringing while I fix these blankety-blank lights that won't light? How about a big kiss to inspire me? Mmmm—Oh! Oh! We almost knocked the tree over.

Hurrah, the lights are working. Aren't I wonderful? Master Electrician Malley.

I'll stand on a chair and place the ornaments you hand me where you want them. You're the big boss and can run the whole shooting match. I'm just your humble stooge but can you guess how you're going to pay me for being so amenable? Quiet, Kathie, how spoiled you've become.

Barbara, don't you think that we should have just a little drink while we string all this popcorn? We simply *must* get this well organized to impress Santa on his first visit to the Malleys'.

Oh, Barbara darling————

But I stood firm.

Monday night
January 6, 1941
Coral Gables

To Eddie

Dearest—

I am sorry if my lawyer's letter was a shock to you. The main reason I want the divorce to be final by the time you come is that I'm weak, darling. Right now, I am very susceptible to seduction. I need a divorce to protect me.

The cocktail napkins arrived. I especially liked the one with the smudge of lipstick on it. Yes, I really appreciated that—you heel! I stay at home and mope all vacation while you go out with beautiful women. 'Tain't fair! Well, me to my books and you to your blondes. . . .

Eddie stood firm, too.

Friday
January 31, 1941
Boston

From Eddie

Dearest Babs,

Divorce or no divorce, I am coming to Florida. I want a vacation; I want to see my baby; and I want to see you. I still have hope that you'll see the life we could have together with a pretty house, tropical fish, love, and a lot of little Malleys.

February 11, 1941
Coral Gables

Eddie is coming a week from Saturday. It's a good thing he is; I feel on the verge of a breakdown. I've been studying for hours every day—working to keep from thinking.

Wednesday
February 12, 1941
Boston

From Eddie

My darling,

I want *you*, I want a *home*, and I want *Kathie* and by God, nothing is going to stop me. So, my love, pile up the sandbags, load up the cannon, and prepare the breastworks; on February 22, the Siege of Barbara will be in its twenty-sixth month and in a renewed state of assault. In the words of Farragut, "I've only just begun to fight."

Thursday
February 13, 1941
Coral Gables
To Eddie

My darling—
   You're going to have an unpleasant shock when you see me. I'm exhausted. I've lost almost ten pounds, so when you step off the train, be on the lookout for a walking skeleton.
   But Kathie is in the pink. I wish you could have heard our duet this afternoon. She would squeal, then I would squeal to encourage her, and then she would reply. Our child is going to be a prima donna. She clasps her hands melodramatically against her cheeks, opens up that rosebud mouth and lets loose.

Wednesday
February 19, 1941
Boston

From Eddie

My dearest darling,
   Just three more days! I wonder how you will greet me. Will you be warm? Eager? Cold? Distant? Coy? Or maybe even with a little love in your heart?

   Ed's letters to me and mine to him stop there; and my diary has a long gap. But I remember what happened next as clearly as if forty-nine years had not elapsed.
   I stood at the station with Kathie in my arms. I wondered what her reaction would be to a daddy she hadn't seen in four months. What would mine *be?*
   Ed stepped out of the train pale, thin, a stranger in his

new blue suit. Both he and I were trembling as we walked to the car. We didn't know what to say to each other.

Kathie saved the day. She ducked her head against my shoulder, then looked up at Ed and grinned. She was flirting with him. I was proud and Ed was won.

That night, alone in the house, Ed kissed me. My dikes burst. All the pent-up emotions of those months without him poured out of me. I wept. I sobbed.

We spent the week basking on the beach. I phoned my lawyer, who assured me we wouldn't have to get married again; just living together would dissolve the interim divorce decree.

We headed north by boat—our honeymoon, with Kathie along. Eddie's father met us at the pier; and when he saw Eddie fumbling with his empty wallet, he pulled out two dollars for the tips.

I never did, of course, return to college, although the rule about married women changed after the war. I had no time to look back. Our second child, Teddy, was born in 1942, followed by Vonnie in 1945 and Timmy in 1946.

September 6, 1947
Cohasset

Last night Ed and I piled all our letters and my diaries in the fireplace to burn them. But we started browsing, and reading choice passages out loud—and after that, neither of us could light the match. So we stored them away in a closet. Perhaps they will combust spontaneously.

When Kathie and Teddy and Vonnie and Timmy are old enough to understand, they may enjoy reading about That Crazy Older Generation.

Michael and his grandfather, 1965.

March 30, 1965
Cohasset

I've been wondering how Ed would accept his new role. The answer is, he hasn't. He refuses to be a grandfather. We've shared many experiences in the past, good, bad, exciting, scary, some requiring no small amount of cajolery on my part, like the time I talked him into dancing lessons at Arthur Murray's. But when it comes to grandparenthood, I've never known him to be so stubborn. I'm on my own, he says.

I've decided not to press the issue. I admire his spirit. If he doesn't want to be a grandfather, he doesn't have to.

June 29, 1965
Cohasset

Vonnie dropped Michael off for a few hours last night. Ed read the paper while I gave the baby his six o'clock bottle.

Then I improvised a bed in the bathtub, tucked him in, and started dinner. When I returned to the living room, who was propped up in Ed's lap, all smiles, but our three-month-old cherub.

"I heard him crying, so I went upstairs to see what was wrong," Ed said. "When I picked him up, I said, 'Your mean grammy put you to bed too early, didn't she.'"

"And what did he say to that?" I asked.

"He said I was exactly right and he likes me best," Ed said smugly.

"Better," I said, correcting his grammar.

"Oh, you noticed it, too."

When Michael began to fuss again, Ed decided he needed burping. "Remember the time Timmy spit up in my pocket and I went to work smelling funny? I've smartened up since then." He produced a hand towel and cradled Michael on his shoulder.

Half an hour later I said, "Do you want your dinner or are you going to play with the baby all night?"

"I'll be there in a minute," Ed said. "Michael says he's ready for bed now." Indeed, the baby had conked out in Ed's arms and was snoring softly. "Smart kid, that grandson of mine."

Five

Great White Eagle
(1962–1970)

March 1, 1962
Cohasset, Massachusetts

Ed is taking flying lessons. When I told Mother the news she cried, "Oh, I *wish* he wouldn't!" I feel the same way, but since he's determined not to let Ted get ahead of him, I can only bow to the inevitable. He has so many responsibilities and so many people dependent on him, I can't help worrying.

I used to think if Ed took up flying, *I'd* want to. Now that I've seen the technical stuff he has to memorize, I've lost interest. If he'll show me how to land the thing in an emergency, I'll feel I know all I need to.

March 30, 1962
Cohasset

Ed and Ted are flying to Florida together tomorrow in Ed's Tri-Pacer. Ed invited me out to dinner tonight: "This is our last night together for almost a week, and I want to be alone with you."

I was so pleased I went upstairs to put on some silver eye

shadow. We had dinner at the Cabin. Ed was in a wonderful mood and kept laughing at all my wry comments—which did wonders for *my* mood.

When we got home Ted latched on to his father ("Hey, Dad, come here and show me how to work this slide rule"), and that was the last I saw of them for two hours. Airplanes, airplanes, you'd think there wasn't another subject in the world. I went to bed in my silver eye shadow and still they talked. At midnight I asked the Flying Malleys if they would please lower their voices.

"Be right up," Ed said.

He couldn't understand what had cooled my ardor. I said querulously—and rather incoherently, I can see in retrospect—that I didn't mind their going to Florida without me, I truly and sincerely thought it was nice for them to have a week alone together. I knew they'd said no females on the trip; but I wasn't a female, I was their wife and mother and not the backseat-driver, yakety-yak type they probably had in mind. Even if they had asked me I wouldn't have been able to go; but just the same, it would have been nice to be asked.

Ed undressed without saying a word, got into bed, pulled the covers up, and said, "Well, ok-unk-ub-bmn-fmph."

"What was that?" I said, beginning to giggle.

"Smartest thing I ever said," Ed replied smugly. "Funniest, too, apparently." Then he fell asleep.

Saturday
March 31, 1962
5:30 a.m.
(groan)
Cohasset

"Ted just checked the weather," Ed said as he woke me up. "We're going to have rain part of the way but it's still—" He mumbled something unintelligible.

Darrell McClure's painting of Plane Deelightful.

"It's still what?" I asked, trying to raise my head from the pillow.

"VFR," he repeated.

"Oh, shut up!" I said.

Ed chuckled.

"I'm going to start talking nothing but Spanish and see how *you* like it," I said.

"You're cute." He came over to kiss me good-bye.

"I expected to see you wearing some sort of gung-ho flying suit," I said.

"It hasn't come yet. Mine has three stripes on the sleeve, Ted's has six."

"Be careful," I said. "Remember to use your turn signals. Don't pass on the right. Dim your lights when approaching another plane. Keep out of the breakdown lane."

Ed headed for the door.

"VFR!" I called, waving jauntily.

"ILS!" he replied.

And off they went into the wide overcast yonder.

Later

Ed just called from Norfolk, Virginia. Because of headwinds, he explained, they'd landed short of their goal.

"Tell her we're going to pick up a couple of girls," I could hear Ted calling from the background.

I *knew* I shouldn't let that pair out of my sight.

Sunday
April 1, 1962
10:30 a.m.
Cohasset

Ed and Ted are still weathered in at Norfolk. Ed is bored and lonely and wishing he hadn't left me behind. Poor Edward. Poor, poor Edward. Oh, goody!

"If you were down here—" Ed began.

"You *miss* me!" I interrupted.

And he's been gone barely twenty-four hours. O happy day!

April 4, 1962
Cohasset

Ed called from Fort Lauderdale, and launched into my favorite subject, Missing Wives:

"Separate vacations are for the birds. I look across the terrace and expect to see you sitting there with your little straw hat, writing in your diary. The nights are the worst. That bed is awfully big and empty and cold."

"So's this one," I assured him.

April 22, 1962
Cohasset

When Ed got home from his flying lesson yesterday, I asked him how he'd done on his cross-country.

"*Terrible.* I was supposed to go west to Southbridge, and I figured the course out and asked the instructor, 'Two hundred eighty-two degrees, right?' Bruce just grunted, and off I went in the wrong direction, one hundred eighty-two degrees. After twenty minutes Bruce gave me a poke and said, 'What's that over there?' I looked and said, 'Must be a lake.' He said it was the Atlantic Ocean. He had let me fly all the way to Fall River, the bastard. I told him he reminded me of the fellow who kept letting his son fall on his head and then warned him, 'Don't trust nobody.'"

I must have looked pained because Ed grinned and said, "Still planning to go up with me this summer?"

"I can hardly wait. Why don't you invite that nice Bruce to come along?"

August 24, 1962
Martha's Vineyard, Massachusetts

We're vacationing at the Vineyard. This morning Ed asked me if I'd like to go flying with him for an hour or so. It was a question I had been nervously anticipating ever since he passed his flight test. He is a "private pilot" now, qualified to carry passengers.

"Why not?" I said. I could think of a dozen reasons why not, none of them marriage buttressing.

My confidence in my husband's new hobby, already flimsy, disintegrated altogether when he had difficulty finding the airport.

"Do we turn here?" he muttered at the Lobster Hatchery sign. "No, I guess it's the next right."

The next right was a dead end. I didn't say a word, but I was thinking in a Jack Bennyish accent: "If he can't find it from the *ground* . . ."

We went back to the Lobster Hatchery sign and turned left—to another dead end, at the lobster hatchery.

"Good for you, I *knew* you could do it!" I said when Great White Eagle, as he now calls himself, eventually located the airport.

Oak Bluffs Airport looked like a reclaimed cow pasture with no runways that I could see. Ed checked the Tri-Pacer's propeller, gas tank, and other essentials; then we climbed in and fastened our seat belts. As he taxied to the end of the pasture I said, "It looks easy. *I* could do that." All at once his hands and feet were pulling levers and pushing pedals and we were roaring toward a grove of trees at ninety miles an hour and I changed my mind. We flew to Nantucket, where Great White Eagle decided to land, "just for practice." A voice on the radio told him which runway to use, and Ed started his approach.

"First time I've ever made a right-hand pattern," he remarked. I said I wished he wouldn't tell me these things.

"Nothing to it," he said, keeling the horizon over on its side and slowing the engine almost to a stall. We landed safely and, since it seemed silly to fly all the way to Nantucket without doing *something*, I went to the ladies' room. Ten minutes later we were ready to take off again.

"Five zero zulu," Ed radioed the tower as he taxied toward the runways. "Do I make a left turn here?"

"Affirmative."

"I'm not too proud to ask," Ed explained to me. "Gave everybody heart attacks last week when I turned the wrong way."

Ed let me fly the plane for a few minutes. (*Let* me? He was tuning the radio in front of my knees. *Someone* had to fly the bloody thing.) I had a tendency to climb. Ed kept telling me to bring the nose down, but my stomach doesn't *like* to bring the nose down. My stomach has a passion for altitude.

As we neared the coastline, Ed descended to a thousand feet and circled Oak Bluffs Harbor. Below us, the *Vineyard Queen* chugged toward the dock, a toy-sized boat trailing a miniature wake. Matchstick figures milled about on the deck, waving to their matchstick friends onshore. I preened my feathers and thought, "Poor earthlings! What a slow way to travel! How confined! How dull!"

Ed found his way back to the Oak Bluffs Airport with no need to stop and ask directions and we coasted gracefully to earth. Thus ended, uneventfully, my flight as Great White Eagle's first passenger.

September 24, 1962
Cohasset

We took a scenic tour over Cohasset and Scituate yesterday afternoon, and Ed gave me more pointers on the art of flying.

I still get butterflies when he lets me take the controls, but I'm beginning to think a few lessons someday might be fun.

Saturday
October 13, 1962
Cohasset

We slept on the boat last night. Ed got up at 7:30, stuck his nose out, and said, "Brrr, it's freezing! Let's go home."

"What do you want to go home for? We just got here."

"Great day for flying," he said.

We argued ("I want to go home," "I want to stay here"), but in the end I gave in, as I always do once a year on Edward's birthday. We began the depressing chore of emptying bureaus and lockers. Ed says we'll be back, but I know better. Goodbye, dear boat. Sob.

But there will be other summers, and fall isn't a bad season, what with Ted's football games at Colby and hot dogs and foliage. We stopped at the house to stow our boating gear and then drove to the airport.

December 10, 1962
Cohasset

Yesterday, the twenty-fourth anniversary of our first meeting, was a black day from beginning to almost the end. We have always celebrated December 9 instead of our wedding anniversary, considering it more romantic; but yesterday went by without so much as a card from the beast.

It wasn't that he was oblivious. He had asked me several times during the week what I wanted, and I kept telling him to ask our new housekeeper; Mrs. Wright knew all the things we needed for the house. He said he wanted to get me something personal. I said, "Honey, I have three hundred pairs of earrings but no soup spoons." Then he forgot. It wasn't *really* important, I told myself. The important thing was how dear and kind and thoughtful he was 364 days a year. I must count my blessings, not give him a hard time. So I cried and cried and gave the poor man an *awful* time. It was my blue devils time of the month, anyway, and watching *The Wizard of Oz* on TV always makes me cry.

Edward was ever so regretful, but I was determined that no one was going to stop me from being miserable. I gave him the anniversary card I had picked out for *him* and said I had meant what it said at the time I picked it out, but now I took it all back. When we went upstairs, I was still sniffling to myself and bemoaning my unloved fate. All at once he held out his arms and said with a tenderness that made me go wishy-washy inside, "Come into my arms, love. Let me comfort you." I did as I was told, though why he wanted to make love to such a red-eyed, puffy-faced ninny, I can't imagine.

December 26, 1962
Cohasset

We celebrated Christmas in Cohasset this season, instead of Florida, and my, how things have changed in three years. Instead of dragging us from our beds at daybreak, according to time-honored custom, our lazy children slept on and on until we finally had to get *them* up.

I took pains to prepare an extra-special breakfast—grilled sausages, scrambled eggs, and my holiday coffee cake. I used our best tablecloth and real silverware, and after the table was set, happily summoned everyone to the dining room.

Vonnie's scowling observation, as Ed began to serve: "*What?* Only two measly sausages apiece?"

"Vonnie," I said, with what I thought was commendable forbearance, "it's Christmas. How about trying to be a little more charming and agreeable than you were yesterday?" I had forgotten one of the cardinal rules governing the relationship between parents and teenagers: Parents Are Not Allowed to Have Feelings. Vonnie disappeared. We waited.

Breakfast was delicious, though barely warm by the time she returned.

In the afternoon Ed and I flew to the Cape to deliver Grandpa and Tina's presents. Ed had trouble getting the engine to turn over, but, after much priming and coaxing it, managed. As we were taking off, he remarked, "It's hard to start the thing in cold weather, but once it starts, it usually keeps going."

Why couldn't we just *mail* our packages, I asked myself, the way other people do?

January 11, 1963
Cohasset

"All I want is to learn to land the thing in an emergency," I explained to Bruce Pronk as he took me aloft for my first formal flying lesson.

But within half an hour I was hooked. What a wonderful feeling it was to handle the Tri-Pacer myself, to discover how obediently it would turn, glide, or climb when I followed Bruce's directions. How exciting it was to be learning something again, to shake the mothballs from my brain and set it to *thinking*.

When I described my first lesson to Ed last night, he noted with a lift of his eyebrows that the Tri-Pacer had suddenly become "*our* plane."

January 13, 1963
Cohasset

Ed has given me his blessing and his bible, Kershner's *Pilot's Flight Manual*. While I was tossing a salad with my free hand, I read aloud to him a passage about the turn-and-bank indicator: "One of the most valuable maneuvers in coping with bad weather is the one-hundred-eighty-degree turn, or 'getting the hell out of there.'" A pair of arms slipped around my waist and a voice addressed the back of my neck.

"I love you," Ed said, giving me a squeeze, "you three-hundred-sixty-five-degree person, you."

"Three hundred sixty-five degrees?"

"Okay, three-sixty. You're learning."

A 180-degree turn put me in a better position for continuing this conversation, a maneuver I accomplished with maximum (110 percent) dexterity.

January 23, 1963
Cohasset

Last Sunday Ed invited me to come along and kibitz while he had an instrument-flying lesson. He had told me a great deal about a plane he'd been using for the last couple of weeks, a Comanche, describing its retractable gear, propeller control, and fuel system, but neglecting to tell me one interesting detail that I discovered myself. When I climbed into the back seat, my eyes fell on a framed document. The name Malley attracted my attention, and when I read the words "Registration Certificate," I put two and two together.

All I said was "*Ohhhhh?*" That was enough.

"Huh?" Ed said, looking at the certificate with a guilty small-boy expression. "You mean the registration?" I could see he hoped I meant something else, like a run in my nylons, maybe.

"Well, I was *gonna* tell you," he said finally, "but I wanted you to see the plane first. Gee, aren't you the smart one to figure it out! Boy, leave it to you to catch on right away. Who else would look at a little paper like that and know right off what it meant!"

"It's a little late for objections," I said, proceeding to enumerate mine, anyway. I was just getting used to the Tri-Pacer, I complained, and now he had to spring this Comanche on me. What was wrong with the Tri-Pacer, anyway? Not fast enough, Ed said. Why did he always have to be in such a hurry? But honey, in this baby we can start in the morning and get to Fort Lauderdale in time for a late-afternoon swim. I like a *small* plane, I said. This thing is too big and complicated; I'll never learn to fly it. Ed said of *course* I'd learn to fly it; if *he* could learn, I could.

I said now I understood why he had been so nice to the draperies salesman last Saturday, with a new Comanche up his sleeve.

"Wasn't I the simpleton!" I continued. "All those piles of literature about Comanches lying around, and I never tumbled."

"You're really adjusting to this very well," Ed said. "In fact, you're being such a good sport, I've decided to forgive you."

February 26, 1963
Cohasset

I never expect to pilot Ed's Comanche, but at least I'm learning to fly a Colt. I won't count the fifteen or twenty landings I made this morning with my instructor's help (I mean like "*Help!*"); but I'm finally beginning to sense when I should level off, and I can *feel* the plane flare out as it settles down like a swan settling on the surface of a pond. W-a-a-y back with the stick, and hallelujah, I've done it.

I grinned at Bruce, who grinned back and said, "That was it—*dee-lightful.*" *Deelightful.* What a perfect name for an airplane.

I felt like a woman who has just learned that the one she loves feels the same about her. I was in love with the Colt, and suddenly, incredibly, it was responding.

April 4, 1963
Cohasset

Tuesday, April 2, was The Day. I've *done* it, I thought, as I drove back to Cohasset. I've flown an airplane into the sky all alone, and I've brought it and myself safely back to earth. For someone who hadn't known how to fly a kite three months ago, this was an achievement. If you crossed a Cheshire cat with the cat that ate the canary, you'd have my expression as I walked into the house and propped my solo certificate up on the mantelpiece.

August 12, 1963
Cohasset

Ed's poor Comanche lies damaged beyond repair in the hangar at Oak Bluffs.

We had flown over to the Vineyard on Saturday and were coming in for a landing at Oak Bluffs. There was nothing unusual about our approach. Everything was in order as we glided toward the field—gear down, full flaps, airspeed okay. Then something inexplicable happened. A gust of wind, or perhaps a downdraft, or a gremlin, caused the plane to plummet instead of continuing its glide.

The exclamation "*Throttle!*" leapt to my lips, but Ed was already pushing it in with a calm forward motion that should have produced the welcome sound of *power*. Instead, the motor failed to catch, and we continued to fall. Our wheels hit the overhang of the sand trap between the field and the golf course and sheared off. We crashed hard and spun 180 degrees.

The force of the spin threw Ed against the windshield, breaking his dark glasses and giving him a deep gash over his right eye. The metal lever on his seat belt hadn't held. My belt, too, gave way. As the plane jarred to a stop, Ed saw me flying headlong through the door, which had burst open.

"Barbara, are you all right?" Ed was standing on the wing of the plane, blood streaming down his face but obviously still alive.

"Yes, I'm all right. My God, what about *you?*"

"I'm okay, it's just a cut, but the plane—my beautiful plane . . . Goddammit, that's the end of the flying, that's the end of airplanes!"

I climbed stiffly to my feet and found I could walk all right except that my shorts kept falling down; the zipper had broken. Ed's face still dripped.

"It's nothing," he said. "But oh, my poor airplane, my beautiful airplane! What happened? What did I do wrong?"

People were swarming around us, asking if we were all right, arguing over who would take us to the hospital.

"Here's the truck, come on, you two," said the greens-keeper. Someone had given Ed a handkerchief to hold against his head; it was already bright red. "You're going to need a few stitches, fella."

"All I need is a safety pin," I said, holding on to my shorts.

From his cot in the hospital's emergency room, Ed gave me my orders. "Call the house, call the insurance company— here's Bill Gail's card; if he isn't home, call the Washington office—call the hotel and tell Timmy to come and get us."

"You lie still," the nurse said, sponging off his face and giving him some gauze pads to staunch the blood. "Press hard."

I went to make the phone calls. When I came back, Dr. Rappaport took me aside. "I'd like him to stay overnight, but I don't suppose he'll listen to you, either. He's quite a manager, that husband of yours. Told me how and where to put the stitches, how to take the X rays, develop them, analyze them . . . Rather used to having things done his way, I should imagine."

Ed said he wanted to go home, climb into bed, pull the covers over his head, and not see or talk to anybody. I kept reminding him of how lucky we were to be alive, how terrible it would have been if one of us had lost the other or if the plane had burst into flames.

"I'm not concerned with what *could* have happened, all I know is what *did* happen. My beautiful plane is a wreck. Flying meant so much to me and now it's all over."

"It doesn't have to be all over. You don't give up driving if you have an automobile accident. As far as I'm concerned, flying is still safer than driving a car."

"Maybe I'll fly again someday. But I'm not going to risk *your* life again."

I told him to stop talking nonsense. "You're a good pilot and you know it. I'm just as confident in you as I ever was— I'd go up with you again tomorrow."

"Well, you're not going to, so forget it."

August 13, 1963
Cohasset

Ed called from Detroit, pleased and excited. First, the insurance company will give us a 1963 Comanche as fully equipped as the one we lost. Second, he is having an interview with a bigwig from the Ford company. There's a good chance of landing a contract making automobile parts.

August 14, 1963
Cohasset

Bruce gave me a lesson in a rented Comanche. I admitted that I was having a delayed case of the jitters. Bruce suggested we break out of the pattern and fly around for a while so I'd get the feel of the controls again.

That calmed me. However, it's one thing to feel relaxed with Charles Lindbergh the Second sitting next to me. The real test will come when he climbs out of our new Comanche—Ed decided on a *Twin* Comanche, bigger and faster than the wrecked one—and says, "Okay, pilot, she's all yours."

September 26, 1963
Cohasset

Yesterday I finally soloed in the Twin Comanche. After I landed, Ed joined me and we flew down to Marshfield together. My generous husband, my *brave* husband, allowed me to be pilot in command. The visibility was terrible on the return trip, so locating Norwood was difficult.

"Don't ask me," said Ed, sitting back with a smug expression. "You're the pilot."

Using the Blue Hill as a guide, I found the airport but was faced with a final approach into a blinding setting sun and a lively crosswind from the south. Made a rather good landing, I thought, but no one would guess it from the way Ed carried on in front of the airport gang.

"Oh, it was awful," he said, staggering into Bruce's office and clutching his head. "What a terrifying experience! Heaven protect me from women drivers."

That's Great White Eagle's way of saying he's proud of me.

November 14, 1963
Cohasset

The first leg of our trip home from Florida was VFR; but, as predicted, the weather closed in just before we reached New York.

I had never flown at night, so I was doubly nervous when the gray swirling mists around us turned pitch-black. All we could see was the dimly lit instrument panel and the red and green lights flashing on our wingtips. Eerie. We had to read our charts and operate the radios with the beam of a flashlight. I panicked when Ed mislaid this vital tool; but, forehanded man that he is, he had a spare in his flight bag.

The ceiling at Norwood was 600 feet, the minimum allowable for an ADF approach. Ed followed the ADF needle to the airport, and when it swung 180 degrees, indicating that we had passed the homer, he began his descent through the inky darkness. Nine hundred feet, 800, 700 . . . a few scattered lights became faintly visible, but no sign of the double row of lights outlining the runway. Six hundred feet . . . no runway.

"Let's not bump into the Blue Hill," I said uneasily as Ed pushed in the throttles and climbed back into the gloom.

He reported the missed approach to Boston Tower.

"What is your intention now, sir?"

"I'm going to try again."

Two visions were batting around in my mind. In one, I was telling the bridge club about our hair-raising landing at Norwood; in the other, someone else was sitting in my chair and Sally was saying, ". . . and I hear the bodies were burned beyond recognition."

The second approach was perfect. What a relief to see those lights materialize through the murk, beckoning us to safety. Moments later the Comanche settled on the runway.

"Never again!" I said. "I'll fly with you in instrument weather and I'll fly at night, but the combination is a bit too much."

"The only way I'll learn is to do these things," Ed said.

I said I'd rather not be in the classroom while he was learning—but he could count on me as a fair-weather friend.

December 2, 1968
Fort Lauderdale, Florida

To my sister, Janeth

I need your advice. Do you think a woman should stay married to a man like this:

We flew to Fort Lauderdale last week in *Plane Deelightful*. I woke up early today feeling very amorous on accounta these sexy dreams I'd been having. Knowing Ed has a marvelous way of making one's dreams come true, I thought I'd see what he had to suggest. Then I remembered he had an early morning fishing date with Alden. Shucks! But what was this sound? Pitter patter of the rain: maybe he wasn't going to go fishing, maybe he was still asleep awaiting the kiss of a beautiful young maiden. (He can dream, too, can't he?) So I rolled over and sure enough, there was this big lump in the other bed, namely my prince. The small lump was Miette, but I wasn't interested in her at the moment.

I nudged Ed awake and proceeded to tell him in detail about my dreams, adding enough embellishments to make Hugh Hefner jump out of his skin.

. . . .

[short passage of time]

Ed: "This sure beats fishing in the rain."
Me, thinking it over: "How about fishing in the sunshine?"
Ed: "Oh . . . about fifty-fifty."

So what is your advice, Jan? Do I hang on to this gem for another thirty years, risking rapid aging due to laugh wrinkles, or do I—or do I—damned if I can think of an acceptable alternative.

November *10*, *1969*
Cohasset

I loved the modest Tri-Pacer in which I took my first few lessons nearly seven years ago. I loved the slightly more advanced Colt, which helped me earn my license. I learned to love our much more advanced single-engine Comanche. I even learned to love our challenging and sophisticated Twin Comanche; but yesterday Ed and I took her aloft for a farewell flight. When we landed, I gave her right engine a sentimental embrace that left, directly over my heart, an indelible imprint of crankcase oil.

Also indelible were those memories of a thousand happy hours in *Plane Deelightful*. When we got her, Ed had vowed that a Twin Comanche was all the airplane a man could ever want. Whatever had now possessed him to part with a friend who had served us so well?

We flew commercial to Denver to examine a plane Ed was planning to buy from Jim Morton of Combs Aircraft. I decided en route I'd better quit my grousing and shape up, or Captain Malley might start shopping around for a new copilot, too.

The stewardess brought our lunch, and with a resigned sigh, I asked Ed to tell me about the turbocharged engines in the plane we were flying two thousand miles to look at. The old axiom on how to fascinate a man (question him about his favorite hobby) remained true; for the rest of the flight I held Ed spellbound while he described the plane's radar, built-in oxygen system, boots, prop deicing, and above all, her fantastic *speed*.

Jim Morton met us at the terminal and drove us to the Combs Aircraft hangar. It was filled with enormous planes; one of them dwarfed all the others.

"There she is," Jim said.

At first I thought he was joshing. Okay, I said, he'd shown us what a supersonic transport looked like; where was this Cessna Skyknight 320 Ed wanted to buy?

"That's it," Ed said. "Boy, she's a beauty, Jim."

"Honey, it's too *much* airplane," I wailed. "I could never learn to fly anything that big. Don't they have a Tri-Pacer around?"

January 16, 1970
Cohasset

The Skyknight landed today at our local airport. Ten little green men landing from Mars couldn't have caused more commotion. Ed dropped everything he was doing in the office; I did the same at home; fifteen minutes later we barely avoided a head-on collision as *he* hurried down the walk to Norwood's transient area just as *I* approached, nose down, from the opposite direction.

Knowing my husband rather well after thirty years, I could see he was in a dither. He turned to the personable young man who had flown the Skyknight in from Denver and said, "Sorry, I'm terrible about names—you're Paul . . . ?"

"Pete Rueck."

"And my name is . . . ," I prompted Ed, hoping he would remember.

"Oh, yes, this is—uh—Barbara. Barbara Malley. My wife."

"How do you like her?" Pete asked, pointing to the blue-and-white behemoth.

Her color scheme was similar to *Plane Deelightful*'s, but there the resemblance ended. Clearly Ed's tales to his friends about the "Baby Airliner" he was expecting had been understated. This was no baby; it was fully two stories tall. Did my husband seriously believe that he—or I?—could fly this Gargantua?

Ed whistled when he saw the instrument panel, and I felt faint. When my vertigo passed, I opened my eyes. They were all still there: switches, buttons, knobs, levers, dials, gauges, and navigational instruments not by the dozen but by the gross. Maybe Ed thought they came cheaper that way. The communication switches alone were enough to make one's head spin: a bristling row of identical white buttons that looked like barracuda teeth. All a pilot had to do was figure out which ones to push in which direction to operate which radio in order to communicate with ground facilities, make an ADF or Omni approach, and utilize such aids as the Marker Beacon, DME, and Electric Horizon. It was too much. By the time I learned how to call HELP on 121.5, it would surely be too late. I decided to mount my pilot's license in a scrapbook and take up needlepoint.

January 17, 1970
Cohasset

"What's the kid's name again?" Ed asked distractedly this morning on our way back to the airport. "George? Harry? Frank?"

"Pete. Pete Rueck."

"Did you say his name's Pete?" Ed asked again as he parked next to the hangar and waved cheerfully to young Mr. Rueck.

"*He* said it. Don't go by me," I replied grouchily. I lagged behind while Ed hastened eagerly toward his new airplane. It had grown both taller and broader during the night, I noticed, and was glaring balefully at me in the winter sunshine.

"I don't like you either," I muttered, climbing into the back seat. I wished I knew how to put her on automatic pilot and let her fly herself back to Colorado, empty. *I* would never fly her. If Ed called this mutiny, so be it.

"Now, easy with those throttles, Ed," Pete said as we rolled down the runway. "Remember, this one's a lot heavier than the Comanche; she glides like a rock."

Ed made two landings Pete's way, but the third time he reverted out of habit to his Comanche technique. *R-r-r-umph!* "See what I mean?" Pete said.

Ed made the next landing Pete's way. "I've got the idea now," he said. "Another couple of hours and I'll have the old girl mastered."

Which reminded him. "How about you, Barb?"

"Yes, master?" I asked, as if I didn't know what was coming.

"Want to give it a try? Nothing to it!"

My distrust of the Skyknight was temporarily overcome by curiosity. I slid into the pilot's seat, and managed not to over-boost on takeoff. Pete talked me all the way down, while I, of course, talked back.

"That's fine, Mrs. Malley, everything's looking good."

"Aren't we too low? Shouldn't I raise the nose? Don't we need more power?"

"No, don't touch a thing, everything's perfect."

[He was right. Unfortunately, I wasn't able to make another landing like it for six months.]

Much as I might regret it, I decided, our Twin Comanche was gone forever. There was no way Ed could wrap up the Skyknight and send it back to the store, so why didn't I face reality and make the adjustment gracefully? Gratefully, even. A husband generous enough to share his Skyknight should be appreciated, not henpecked. From now on, I promised myself, I would stop giving Ed a hard time.

August 12, 1970
Cohasset

A couple of weeks ago, not having a computer handy, I counted on my fingers. We had traded the Comanche in on the Skyknight last November . . . good grief, it was nearly nine months since I'd flown an airplane alone. This was a pause altogether too pregnant. I would have to stop stalling and start producing or there'd be a lot of raised eyebrows in the family.

"How're you doing with the new plane, Mom?" Ted and Tim have been asking.

"Well, I don't hate it anymore," I conceded. "In fact, I'm beginning to enjoy flying again now that I can get her down without bouncing. A few more good landings . . ."

Both Ed and my instructor, Silky Sullivan, have been telling me for weeks that I was free to take off alone any time I felt like it. Well, I didn't feel like it. I had a sore shoulder, the garden needed weeding, and anyway, the weather was always too hot, too windy, or too hazy for me to face the nerve-racking challenge of soloing in Ed's Baby Airliner. How could a 122-pound weakling who couldn't even reach the gas tanks without standing on an orange crate possibly be expected to start up those big engines single-handed, taxi out to the active runway, and go through a series of complicated procedures that would inexorably lead to a condition known as airborne? One could not become "a little bit airborne" and then change one's mind. There was a traffic pattern to be reentered, a landing to be accomplished.

Accomplished landings, that was all I asked. Silky and Ed might think I was adequately prepared, but the inner needle that measured my self-confidence was still giving a negative indication. Perhaps I'd work up the nerve during our vacation in August.

"S-a-a-y!" Ed said last weekend, as our two-and-a-half-ton Skyknight touched the Martha's Vineyard runway as delicately as a butterfly. "What's happened? That's the third grease job you've done in a row."

Barbara, Skyknight, and Great White Eagle, 1970.

"I kept the power on all the way. You've been doing the same thing lately, and I noticed it seemed to give you more control over your landings. I thought what worked for you might work for me."

"That must be the answer. Up until now this airplane has been flying you, but all of a sudden you've started flying her."

"I have to admit you were right, she's easier to land than the Comanche," I said, blushing at this heresy to my dear departed.

With my nerve-measuring needle registering well into the green, the thought of taking off alone had lost its terrors. The next morning Ed accompanied me on two trips around the pattern, then said, "You've got it made, kid; be sure the door is closed tightly," and out he got.

I taxied onto runway 33 with about as much trepidation as a housewife driving to the corner grocery store.

"Okay, sweetheart," I said to my former archenemy. "It's a hot day and a short runway and there's trees in them thar woods. Let's not fool around."

Raise the nose at ninety, lift off a little sooner than usual, lower the nose slightly to build up airspeed. What a good, obedient girl she was! Why had I found her so intimidating?

As I turned toward final I gave myself my Missed Approach Lecture.

"Just because you're on final, remember there's no law that says you *have* to land. If you don't like the way things look down there, you can always go around again."

Having attended my lecture, I forgot about it and began concentrating on making the most beautiful landing in history for my husband. Not that I wasn't aware of the airplane sitting at an angle on the left side of the runway; I just assumed he was aware of me.

Actually, the only aware person in the vicinity was Ed, whose hair stood on end when he saw the pilot taxi beyond the yellow run-up line and, without a glance at the incoming traffic (me!), casually begin his run-up. Ed ran toward him, yelling and gesticulating, but was unable to get his attention. As the Skyknight crossed the barrier, the smaller plane moved toward the center of the runway. Suddenly the pilot's head jerked upward and he braked sharply. It took a large unidentified flying object directly over his head to convince him this wasn't his own private runway.

Ed had recuperated by the time the Skyknight hummed down to that perfect landing. When I taxied her back to the parking area, he was clasping both hands in the air and doing a celebratory jig, oblivious to the stares of passengers boarding a nearby aircraft.

I jumped out of the plane, threw my arms around my husband, and said, "Mmmmm, I love you!"

"I'll bet you say that to all your instructors," Ed said.

Then I patted the new *Plane Deelightful* and told her I loved her, too.

Six

The Letter, the Loony Bin, and Letting Go
(1970–1971)

December 9, 1970
Fort Lauderdale, Florida

I found a letter.

Like countless other wives, I found a letter. Without my reading glasses, I could see only the kisses at the end and thought it was one of mine. Then I saw Ed standing in the doorway. His face told me everything.

I have been as naive as any other last-to-know wife.

I thought I had imagination enough to keep myself interesting and desirable to my husband in and out of bed. But there was one element I could not provide: a different body. One woman is not enough for him and, it seems, hasn't been enough for years.

I feel as obliterated as a figure erased from a blackboard. Life stands still. I have nothing. I *am* nothing. What do I do at age forty-nine—go out on the nearest street corner and announce my new status? "Hey, you fellows who used to dance close and tell me I was sexy, guess what, I'm available!"

It's too late. I'm too old. Who can see or hear an obliterated figure?

Ed has flown back to Boston. Like an automaton I drove him to the airport. I watched him start up his plane. Why didn't I run out in front of it to stop him? Today is our thirty-second anniversary. . . .

January 7, 1971
Graystone Hospital
Boston

Will it help? Will it help to preserve my sanity in this hellhole if I use this "weapon" (dear, familiar, comfortable pencil), which I am at last allowed to have? Yes, it helps. Already I feel the taut, frightened muscles in my stomach relax as words flow from brain to pencil point to paper.

I was here for two or three days before I realized that the burly attendants patrolling the ward are not nurses but custodians. It is not part of their job to be gentle or sympathetic. Their vigilance consists of seeing to it that we suicide freaks don't make another attempt—not on *their* shift.

I wasn't permitted a phone call—not even to my mother—during the first forty-eight hours. I wonder what logic dictates this insane rule. When does a human being have more need for the sound of a caring voice than at this critical moment—plucked from death's door, perhaps, but still emotionally poised on the threshold? The authorities seem to be saying: "You attempted to kill yourself. You must be punished for this crime."

Yes, I will think twice if I ever escape from here. I'll con my psychiatrist and talk my way out. Then, if suicide still seems the only alternative, I'll make very sure I don't bungle the job a second time.

Gina, the girl-man, is locked in the seclusion room today. She arrived three days ago, and ever since the door clanged behind her, she has been frightening the rest of us with her violent attempts to escape. Night before last she seized a chair in her muscular arms and smashed the "shatter-proof" window in the side exit. It took two husky custodians to subdue her.

After she quieted down, Gina leaned against the door with her shaggy head hanging through the opening created by the flung chair, breathing in the freedom that lay beyond. The repairman arrived. Gina paced restlessly as the new window was inserted from the other side of the door, and nails were hammered home. The task was nearly completed when she rushed at the door and roared, *"No more nails! No more nails!"*

Lois is a tall, strongly built woman with a sinister face and unkempt yellow hair issuing from brown roots. She marches up and down the corridor outside the wards, her eyes narrowed to slits, smiling evilly at some horrible secret. At times her mirth explodes into laughter, which is almost worse to hear than Gina's screams from the seclusion room.

I try not to imagine myself locked up in that room.

Mrs. Hennessey is a skeleton-thin old lady who never feels like eating. The custodian cuts up her food and pushes it into her mouth while threatening, if she doesn't swallow, to have the food ground up and forced down her nose.

Last night I looked at my dinner and felt like gagging at the cold slab of hamburg, the scoop of mashed potatoes, the chunk of lettuce without dressing. Then I thought of Mrs. Hennessey and managed to choke down a few bites.

I drink a lot of milk. Perhaps milk will save my life. My weight yesterday morning was 114 pounds . . . ten pounds lost in ten days—or is it twelve days? I've lost track.

Each night, when the rest of us are getting ready to retire, gray-haired Mrs. Lawson puts on her hat and coat, picks up her suitcase, and announces she is ready to leave.

"Has anyone seen my Dorothy?" she asks, wandering from one ward to the next. One of the first nights I was here, she approached my bed, peered into my face, and gently inquired: "Are you my darling Dorothy?"

January 21, 1971
Westwood, Massachusetts*

Ed pleads for a forgive-and-forget resolution to our rift, but despite his vows that the affair is over and will never happen again, I feel unmoved. To his distress, I have slept in the guest room since my return from the hospital day before yesterday. Ed is threatening to go crazy, too. I wonder how he'll like Graystone. I'll visit him every day and bring him Golden Delicious apples and a file.

"If it's this bad after three days," he said this morning (already he's so addled he can't add one and one), "how am I going to feel after three weeks? I love you. I've never stopped loving you. I need you . . . *now*."

When I proposed that we live as brother and sister for at least a year, his bellow of pain was the kind heard on a farm when they are making a steer out of a calf. Unable to dissuade me ("Can't we discuss this with our clothes off?"), my husband eventually gave up chasing me around the kitchen and then left for the office, murmuring something about sweet torture.

I am not out to punish Edward or even amuse myself with a little friendly sadism. I just don't feel physically toward him the way I used to. Perhaps I will someday, but I can't force emotions that aren't there. Parts of me long to be held and loved, but my real me cries out for something more. The need to know I am desired is more important to me than the con-

---

*Ed and I moved to a small ranch house in Westwood, near Norwood Airport, in October 1966.

summation of desire. To be accused of sweet torture sounds better to my ears than the condescending pat on the head and the comment "You're a nice girl." I don't want to be a nice girl. If I'd wanted to be a nice girl I wouldn't have gotten pregnant at eighteen. (Thirty-one years ago!)

January 24, 1971
Westwood

I have succumbed. But we were not alone, Ed and I. Someone else had joined us, someone whose name and face are unknown to me. Even as my body appeased its hunger, my mind shrank back. She was present for him, too, adding for him a bizarre deliciousness to his lovemaking. I know that he knew that I knew this. How do I drive her from our rites, once so tender and private? Can a vision be assassinated?

March 20, 1971
Westwood

In the past, Ed went out of his way to convince me our marriage was special; he assured me he would never jeopardize it by being unfaithful. When I finally learned the truth, the straying itself was as great a shock as the accompanying deceptions.

"*Why?*" I asked him during one of our many confrontations. "Why did you make such a point of assuring me you were the world's most true-blue husband?"

"Because I'm a male chauvinist, that's why," Ed said. "I didn't want you doing what I was doing."

He knew me well.

Ed also said what men and women always say in defense of their lying: "I didn't want to hurt you." I'm sure this is as true as his male chauvinist statement.

May 25, 1971
Westwood

I'm still desperately trying to accept the unacceptable. Ed has become so bored and irritated with my recriminations that he dreads coming home. I watched through the kitchen window last night when his car pulled to a stop; he sat slumped over the wheel, bracing himself for his entrance into the witch's lair. Where is the husband and lover who used to take the steps two at a time in his eagerness to embrace his darling?

I hate him for transforming me into a witch and then disliking what he has made of me.

My psychiatrist has been no help. Dr. C. is a male chauvinist anachronism who can't understand what all the fuss is about. Marriage has always been this way, he says; why did you expect it to be different for you? But Ed always told me we *were* different. I was special, our marriage was special, he'd never be so foolish as to jeopardize all he held dear.

When I told Dr. Chauvin I was thinking of sampling some forbidden fruits myself, he said, "Society has a name for a woman like that: slut." I have sent him a final check but I still owe him a kick in the groin.

June 2, 1971
Westwood

Ed and I continue to live as man and wife in a traumatized marriage, my emotions seesawing from one day to the next. I try to believe his promises, but I bitterly resent the years of deception. Ed would like to turn back the clock, but I'm not sure that's possible. When trust is shattered, its shards lie too close to the heart.

June 21, 1971
Westwood

I decided recently to try the little blue pills prescribed by Dr. C. It took a few days for them to work. Then, surprisingly, the world began to look brighter. Past injustices no longer seemed worth dwelling on. I feel stronger and thankful to be alive for the first time in months. I take three tablets a day except during my "bad period," when an extra one helps. I'm only sorry I resisted medication so long.

No need to seek out a new psychiatrist. I not only feel more forgiving toward Ed but toward myself, as well. I recognize now that in attempting to end my life I was diverting the rage I felt toward him back against myself.

I started reading a poem in *A Book of Irreverent Poetry*:

> Hope is looking up
> Hate is looking back
> Love is looking ahead
> Fear is eyes all over your head.

That line stopped me cold.

My darkroom is almost finished. Soon I'll be able to start making enlargements. I'm grateful to Ed for the Nikon.

July 14, 1971
Westwood

My Nikon has been a life preserver. Through its viewfinder, I have given the world a second look and discovered beauty. The hours I spend in the darkroom are enthralling. (But lonely.)

Floyd Rinker, my high school English teacher and continuing mentor, phoned to ask how I was.

"Could be better," I said.

"Come over and tell me about it."

I did. After a few hours of telling him, I asked: "Where do I go from here?"

"How much traveling have you done?"

"Martha's Vineyard. Fort Lauderdale."

"Never been to Europe? At your age? Go!"

I tried to hide my qualms about traveling alone, but this guru read my mind—and bided his time.

"If you'll behave yourself," he said gruffly over lunch a week later, "maybe I'll go along. I don't like to be spoken to until after I've had my morning coffee, I don't like to be kept waiting for cocktails, and don't expect me to traipse all over the countryside with you and your camera."

Included in our travel arrangements are two side tours for me alone: to Copenhagen and to Istanbul.

September 11, 1971
King Frederick Hotel
Copenhagen, Denmark

To Floyd Rinker

After checking into the King Frederick, I walked across the square to the Tivoli Gardens and had my first adventure almost as soon as I passed through the gate. I was taking in all the lights and excitement and fun, and bumping into people in a touristy way that would make Ed cringe, when suddenly I found myself nose to nose with an Indian! I couldn't have jumped back faster if he'd had a tomahawk and feathers. He was the kind of Indian who comes from India; but his swarthy complexion, curly black beard, and gleaming black eyes weren't what I'd expected to meet on a dark night in the Tivoli Gardens.

"Hello," he said, between the gap in his front teeth.

I was speechless.

"I only said hello. Is that so frightening?"

He fell into step beside me, asking where I was from and how I liked Copenhagen. I decided to ignore his piratical appearance and assume he was a harmless foreigner from a strange land, even as I. He told me how difficult it was for a native of India to leave his country. After buying his airline ticket, he was permitted to take with him only eight dollars in American currency. Fortunately, he had a brother living in London, who was able to help him.

"Oh, look," he said, stopping suddenly and pointing. "They have gambling in there. Do you enjoy gambling? Why don't we go in and watch?"

I saw that piratical glint in his eye again, and clutched my purse more tightly. I said I didn't care for gambling and thought I'd go back to my hotel.

He walked me there, and when I wouldn't agree to meet him the next night, he bowed and smiled and said we would perhaps meet again by chance.

If you never hear from me again, you'll know we met by chance, whereupon I was doped and smuggled off to Bombay as a white slave. . . .

Further adventures I'll relate in person when I see you in Venice. Don't plan to meet my train; I have become self-sufficient and will see you at the whatever-it-is hotel when I get there. If I'm more than forty-eight hours late, check with the Bureau of Missing Persons in Bombay.

I have been forgetting to take my tranquilizers, yet have never felt more tranquil. I think of Ed once in a while, but I am no longer obsessed. Your travel prescription is working, Dr. Rinker. . . .

September 13, 1971
Venice

My train was due to arrive in Venice at 5:02 P.M. At 5:05 the train stopped and the few passengers still aboard began

Your travel prescription is working, Dr. Rinker.

piling off. I hefted my two suitcases down from the overhead rack, then discovered the corridor was too narrow and crowded to get everything off in one trip. With my carryall and camera hanging from my left shoulder, and my purse and smaller suitcase clutched in my right hand, I disembarked. Leaving the suitcase on the platform, I returned to my compartment for the jumbo bag. By the time I staggered down the steps of the train, my shoulders were pleading for mercy. Not a porter in sight. Italian male stalwarts who had ogled me moments earlier now stared studiously in other directions.

Loaded like a camel, I staggered down a long flight of stairs leading to the terminal and eventually found a taxi.

"The Bauer-Grunwald Hotel, please," I said to the handsome young driver.

"The Bauer-Grunwald is in Venice."

"I know," I said. "That's where I want you to take me."

"It will cost you thirty thousand lire."

It sounded like a lot of lire.

"Why so much?"

"Because we are not in Venice. You should have gotten off at the next stop."

I pictured myself staggering back to the train, only to have it chug off as I approached. *Quel* nightmare! Okay, I told the driver, take me to the Bauer-Grunwald.

On the way, I remembered my letter to Floyd. Suppose he had disobeyed orders and was now waiting for me at the Venezia station?

"Driver, I may have a friend waiting for me at the railroad station. We'd better go there first."

"I cannot do this, Madame."

"Why not?"

"Because of the canals. I will take you to the water bus that will take you to the station."

At the water bus dock, I dragged, pushed, and pulled my luggage to the ticket window while a throng of muttering commuters shouldered their way past me. I was now sweating profusely and was sure my hairpiece as well as my scarf needed adjusting. Either that or my bangs had grown three inches in ten minutes.

"A ticket to the railroad station," I said when I reached the window.

"*Numero uno, numero uno.*"

"Yes, just one," I said.

"*Numero uno!*" the ticket agent repeated, glaring and pointing off to his right.

I assembled my bags again and dragged them toward gate *numero uno*. I remembered that Kathie's impression of Italian men had been unfavorable, and I was fast learning why. Gallant, charming, and flattering they may be when you're tripping along, hoping you still look good enough to rate a wink; but physical assistance unrelated to lechery is not their forte.

As I joined the crowd milling toward the boat, my purse fell open and spilled out my passport, hotel itinerary, change purse, and vitamin pills. People stepped around, over, and on me while I crouched down to collect my belongings. I was the last one to board the boat.

When I reached the Venezia station neither my train nor Floyd was there. My bangs grew another four inches as I gathered my baggage and took a water bus to the Bauer-Grunwald.

Enough. My pencil is worn to the nub and so am I.

Later

From the moment I reached this hotel, I've been in a fairyland. The Grand Canal flows by my balcony. Across the canal is a church, its dome glowing in the light of the setting sun. Wherever I turn, there are spires, domes, and cupolas outlined against a pink-streaked sky. The activity on the canal holds me like a magnet; I can scarcely tear myself away long enough to unpack. Gondolas, propelled by lithe gondoliers. Open barges, conveying everything from laundry to vegetables. Motorboats, water buses, huge steamships—there is so much to see, it is impossible to describe. Venice . . . ah, Venice! Everyone I love must see Venice.

September 21, 1971
S.S. Galaxy
Istanbul

A week on a cruise ship seems like a year of ordinary living, but we finally arrived in Istanbul day before yesterday. I visited the city's famous bazaar—sixty-seven streets with forty-four hundred shops. I walked quickly through the maze of narrow lanes, bought nothing, but took a few pictures.

The streets beyond the bazaar teemed with sellers, buyers, strollers, beggars, and creatures humped over like camels, bearing enormous burdens on their padded backs. I snapped picture after picture.

Nearby was the university and an open area where handfuls of corn were sold by crones and children. A pretty Egyptian girl assured me I would get my wish if I threw the pigeons a few golden kernels. I threw a few kernels.

A young man, wearing tinted glasses and a dark mustache, spoke to me next.

"You are American. Are you visiting our city for long?"

"No, my ship is leaving day after tomorrow."

"I am a student at the university," he said, falling into step beside me. I hoped he wasn't going to be a pest. I didn't want company, I wanted to take pictures.

The young man introduced himself as Ahmet and continued to ask questions. I hesitated to hurt his feelings by suggesting he get lost.

Ahmet offered to take me to picturesque areas I would have difficulty finding by myself—outdoor markets, fishing wharves, parks. At no charge, he added. "You are a very attractive woman, if you don't mind my saying so."

I didn't mind. I took a picture of him and he took one of me.

Ahmet was twenty-four and couldn't believe I had two

sons almost as old as he. "You are so slim and shapely—surely you must have been a child bride?"

Going, going, gone. At the end of the afternoon, as Ahmet walked me back to my ship, I agreed to meet him after dinner and let him show me Istanbul's nightlife.

I took the precaution of telling shipboard friends that I was going out for the evening with a student named Ahmet.

"If you don't show up for breakfast, we'll sound the alarm," they assured me.

My escort took me first to a shabby café where we had drinks and tried to talk above the clamor of a jukebox. Soon Ahmet was calling me Barbara, clutching my hand in both of his, and vowing I was the most fascinating woman he had ever met. After one more drink, I believed him.

He was not satisfied just to hold my hand, he said. He would take me to a place where there was dancing, so he could hold me in his arms.

The next dive shrouded its seedy atmosphere in darkness. Battered tables, lit by candle stumps, were grouped around a dance floor. We had more to drink, we talked, we danced. Ahmet said I had bewitched him, he couldn't bear to think he would never see me again. Behind his glasses, his hooded eyes entreated me to relax and let him hold me closer.

"You are not afraid of me, are you?" he asked. "You can trust me totally."

So might a cobra speak if it had a larynx and a Turkish accent.

Soon I told Ahmet I should go back to my ship.

"It's too late," he insisted, showing me his watch. "The authorities close the gates to the ship at midnight."

Then I would have to go to a hotel, I told him. I was tired and had had too much to drink, and I really wasn't feeling very well. Ahmet said it was all his fault, he was so enchanted with me that he had lost track of the time.

My stomach rumbled disagreeably. I was beginning to think I had picked up an affliction from one unwashed glass or another.

Now, arguing persuasively, Ahmet convinced me I should spend the night at his home, which he described as a villa, with terraces and landscaped grounds. There, he assured me, I could enjoy complete privacy in a separate apartment; and to prove his honorable intentions, he would give me the key to my bedroom door. He would get me back to my ship first thing in the morning

Several bus changes followed, with the neighborhood and our fellow passengers gradually deteriorating. I felt increasingly alarmed.

"Ahmet, I've changed my mind. I want to go back to the city."

"There are no connections at this hour. Why have you changed your mind, Barbara? Are you frightened? No harm will come to you as long as you are with me."

Next, we were walking down a deserted alley, lined with the dark, irregular shapes of two- and three-decker tenements. I desperately needed a bathroom. That first, then a policeman.

"Here we are," said Ahmet, whose voice had begun to sound brisker and less ingratiating as we neared the home he had described in such splendid terms. He led me down a set of jagged stone steps, took out his key, and pushed open a scarred, creaking door.

"Where is the bathroom?" I asked, looking around the dingy apartment. I had been thoroughly conned. The question was, would I now be killed or was I just in for a bad night?

"Over there." Ahmet pointed to a curtain. "The toilet seat came from Sears, Roebuck," he added with a note of pride. "We haven't had it connected yet, but you can use it."

"*We?*" I asked.

"My cousin, with whom I share these quarters. You remember my telling you about him?"

Yes, I remembered something about a cousin. At the time I had visualized "these quarters" as less intimate.

"He is very nice, you will meet him in the morning. Ah—here he is now."

A dark-skinned youth with sparse black whiskers, pulling on a pair of trousers, came through one of two doors opposite the curtain. Ahmet started to introduce us.

"I have to go to the bathroom," I interrupted.

The toilet seat, backed by a lidless, empty tank, was stationed over a hole in the floor. I had no choice but to use it.

Outside I could hear Ahmet and his cousin conversing in low voices. Oh, God. Trapped in a twelve-by-fourteen "villa" with Bluebeard the Turk and his cousin, Blackbeard!

"Barbara, if you need water, I will show you where you can wash up," Ahmet called through the curtain.

When I came out, the cousin had disappeared. Ahmet said he had gone to bed. I certainly hoped so. He ushered me into a cubbyhole that was apparently the kitchen. There was no sink, just a pipe with a faucet.

"Where's a towel?" I asked.

Ahmet gestured toward a grimy rag hanging next to the pipe and left me to manage my Turkish bath as best I could.

Ahmet entered our cell in his maroon pajamas, removed his glasses, and surveyed me with dark, heavy-lidded eyes. He had transformed himself from a mild-mannered university student to an imperious mustachioed sultan, accustomed to having his way with his choice of the night.

Ahmet said, "Do this." Ahmet said, "Do that." It wasn't a pleasant game, but I played along as meekly as a child. Frightened though I was, I let him know where I drew the line.

In an attempt to think positively, a precept of my mother's,

I tried visualizing myself aboard my ship, having an elegant breakfast with my fellow passengers. If they could see me now . . .

Through that long night I felt an affinity with women of all times and all cultures who have been sexually exploited against their will. How many, I wondered, were as despairing and vulnerable as I?

The next morning, haggard and degraded, my self-esteem in shreds, I accompanied Ahmet and his cousin to the bus stop. The three of us talked about the weather on the long ride back to the city.

September 22, 1971
Departing from Istanbul

It worked again. Like my stay in the loony bin, my night with Ahmet lost its obsessive power once I had written it out in terror-assuaging paragraphs.

I stayed in my cabin on the ship until noon yesterday, writing, writing. I sent for a sandwich and wrote some more. Then I slept, and slept. This evening I was ready to face the pre-dinner cocktail group. There, someone asked me, "What do you do?" I had rarely heard this question until I started traveling. At first, my stammered answer was "I'm a housewife, I guess." But now another answer occurred to me: "Well, for one thing, I fly an airplane."

This terminated all conversations within earshot as effectively as if I'd announced I was a go-go dancer. My shipmates insisted on hearing about some of the zanier adventures Ed and I have had, starting with our boating days; they wouldn't let me stop until my memory ran dry. Next to writing, holding a group's attention is the best poultice for a traumatized psyche.

I am about to go to bed, after condensing a sanitized version of Istanbul and Ahmet onto a postcard for Kathie: "Leaving the bazaar, I was picked up by a twenty-four-year-old Turk, a university student who told me I was beautiful and said he wanted to take me dancing so he could hold me in his arms. Wherever you may roam, a line is a line is a line. After a few drinks of Turkish rotgut, we did go dancing and I woke up next morning with a hangover. Love, Mom."

November 2, 1971
Westwood

I returned from Europe looking and feeling like the one thing I had never been able to be for Ed since 1940—a new woman. His rekindled interest warmed my mending heart but otherwise left me cold. In an earlier era we might have reconciled and lived haphazardly ever after, but now I know I have options besides shrinks, suicide, and little blue pills. I asked Ed for a trial separation.

"'Enry 'Iggins" was sure I'd come crawling back in two weeks as if, like Eliza Doolittle, I was nothing without him. Instead, I have made an unexpected discovery: being single again isn't all that bad. Rather than orbiting like a trapped satellite around my husband's personal planet, I am free to explore new worlds, including the world evolving inside my head.

I have joined a women's consciousness-raising group, and signed up for a seminar for recently divorced and separated women and men. I'm looking into Parents Without Partners. I'm even taking dancing lessons.

Seven

It's Never Too Late to
Live in Sin
(1972–1974)

*During our trial separation Ed rented a house in Co-
hasset, while I remained in Westwood. Although he
dated other women, he continued to court me with
phone calls, letters, and dinner invitations. I embarked
on the dating game, but never encountered a man I
wanted to see a second time until . . .*

July 26, 1972
Westwood, Massachusetts

I have met a man. Not the dashing, younger-than-I suitor I
dreamed of flaunting in front of my wandering husband's
wondering eyes but a tall, gray-haired widower of fifty-two
who doesn't know how to dance (good-bye, mambo, tango,
samba, rhumba; it was fun making your acquaintance). Chris
is courtly, gentle, smells better than the nuzzly spot on a baby's
neck, and is myopically dazzled by my beauty. His invariable

greeting is "When am I going to see you again?" I can't believe what's happening. I love every moment with him.

Ed is still unhappy about our separation. Why is being happy so difficult?

Chris and I shared a couple of joints last night, and I grew profound. I made a soul-stirring pronouncement and waited eagerly for his reaction. He seemed stunned; an eternity of ten or twelve seconds ticked by while he stared at me. Then he said, "*What* in *hell* are you talking about?"

By then I had forgotten.

September 12, 1972
Westwood

My gallant swain is convinced that he has captured not a lady but a tiger. In twenty years of marriage, he and his wife never saw each other with their clothes off! Chris's modesty is so extreme, I suspect he keeps his eyes closed while urinating, whistling aimlessly and hoping for the best.

The first time I asked Sir Galahad to excuse me while I took a leak, he couldn't believe his ears. Never did he dream such a four-letter word would pass the innocent lips of his ladylove. Did I have surprises in store for him! Since I'm not about to change my style for anyone, my knight has had to face reality: *his lady is no lady.*

It's a dull day when I don't hear my name enunciated in italics, double underlinings, and three exclamation points. "*Barbara!!!*" he gasps, reeling from yet another shock to his scatologophobia. The more scandalized he is by my words and phrases, the more I enjoy showing him what else I know.

But there is more to it than that. I feel that of all people in the world, a couple in love should be able to communicate without inhibitions. Why should we refrain from using earthy, expressive language because he is a man and I am a woman? When he is in the company of a male friend who is telling a

It would be a sure way to lose Henry for a while.

bawdy story, surely he doesn't say, "Oh, fie, Ralph, I don't want to hear that kind of thing!"

"That's different," he protests.

He tries his best to understand. "I love my angel who swears and talks dirty," he assures me gallantly.

Rounding out the scanty sex education of this adorable square is more fun than a romp with a virginal lad of nineteen. (Seventeen? Fifteen? What are the latest statistics on virginal lads?) Progress is slow but steady. Sometimes drastic measures are called for, such as my heaving his shorts out of reach when he insisted on donning them after lovemaking. I told him I didn't want any Fruit of the Loom barrier between us, I wanted to feel *him*.

"Honey, would you please get my shorts?"

"No."

"What am I supposed to do, go home without them?"

"Why don't you walk over and get them?"

"But the hall light's on."

"Terrific!"

Whereupon he crawled to his shorts on all fours as if crossing enemy lines under heavy fire.

That sex can be anything but serious hadn't occurred to Chris before he met me. Once, after a glowingly fulfilling session in bed, I said, "That was a hell of a lot of fun!"

To which he replied solemnly, "No, that's not what it was, angel. Fun is playing softball and like that."

After teaching him that his shorts had no tactile appeal for me, I assigned him his next lesson: Taking a Shower Together.

Absolutely not, Chris said. He didn't see the point in such a bizarre idea. He'd never taken a shower with a woman in his life, and he wasn't going to start now. Though an amiable man, he can be stubborn when he makes up his mind. That makes two of us. At last came the breakthrough—and the deluge.

"Isn't this fun?" I asked gleefully.

"Yes," he admitted, as we exchanged warm, watery caresses.

One short week later, the next milestone: *a shower with the lights on*. As we played together under the shower head, laughing and soaping each other's bodies, I felt as triumphant as Eve under the apple tree.

October 13, 1972
Framingham, Massachusetts

To Chris

Querido mío—

I am in the Trailways terminal, waiting for the bus that will take me away from my Chris. Bad bus! A talkative fellow traveler named Henry, who is also en route to Mexico, has just excused himself, explaining that he is going to the *salón de caballeros*. Why he chooses to visit a beauty shop for cowboys at this moment is beyond me, but it is helpful of him to start conversing in Spanish so soon. By the time we get to Acapulco I should be fluent, *no es verdad?*

I'm sorry I missed you when I phoned good-bye this morning. The receptionist offered to take my message, but how could I say "I love you" to a woman I've never met?

Later

I'm in room 6R in the Holiday Inn at Kennedy Airport.

"What did she pack in that suitcase?" my neck bone complains to my shoulder bone, "the Westwood Public Library?"

Henry invited me to join him for a nightcap. I said I was going to take a shower and write a letter (with my pen that writes underwater).

I wish I'd remembered to bring my book of magic spells

with me so I could conjure up something that looks like you and smells like English Leather. Ummmm!

We leave at 9:00 A.M. tomorrow. *Goodness*, how I miss you!

October 18, 1972
El Presidente
Acapulco

To Chris

My Chris,

After such a long separation are you still—yes, of course you are. Now that we have *that* settled . . .

I'm riding toward Acapulco on a tour bus with a guide named Pepe. If we had driven right through, we could have reached our destination in three hours, but thanks to Pepe, we made three stops, ostensibly to use the facilities and have refreshments. In truth, it was to allow more of our Yankee dollars to be extracted by the owners of tourist traps, with Pepe, of course, getting his cut.

Henry and I are sort of paired off. He sits next to me on the bus, consults me on "our" plans for the next day, and follows me around when I'm trying to take pictures. Mexicans are camera-shy, and it's hard enough to charm them into cooperating without Helpful Henry at my elbow. So far I haven't had the heart to be rude to someone who means so well. He's all right, the way scrambled eggs without salt are all right.

I plan to skip the group tour tomorrow and go exploring in the market district. The next day I'll take a parachute ride on the back of a speedboat if I don't lose my nerve. I talked with a girl who had just floated down to the beach (I had been taking pictures of her descent and had to dodge to keep from being landed on), and she said it took her two days and three drinks to work up her courage. It would be a sure way to lose Henry for a while.

I MISS YOU.

November 4, 1972
Westwood

My shock value is beginning to fade. Now when I come out with a word or expression Chris has never heard outside the navy, my name is underlined only once. I rather miss the exclamation points, but the grin he gives me compensates.

My climactic moment was the day he said *his* first bad word. That was one for the memory book.

Discussing how he stormed out after a fight we had last week, he said, "I got home at twenty minutes of ten, still all shaved and fresh. It was the type of thing *you* say 'shit' to. Like the little pig: 'shit-shit-shit all the way home.'"

Steadfastly gallant, my knight has taught *me* a few things about love and sex, too. Last night I looked up at him as we headed toward the bedroom and asked, daring him to give an honest answer, "What do you want to do?"

He pondered the limitless alternatives and then said tenderly, "I want to love you."

Our relationship may sound idyllic, but of course it isn't. We differ in too many ways. My biases are: Darwin yes, God maybe, Nixon no. His are the reverse. He is a hawk, I am a dove. I'm for McGovern, he's for Whatsisname. Whether it's politics, social issues, or the temperature of the water in the shower (he likes it hot, I like it scalding), we argue oftener than we agree. He is adamant about one thing. He wants to keep seeing me, no matter how misguided he thinks my thinking is.

There's one other problem with Chris. He makes me laugh so much that the creases around my eyes are deepening. I've warned him that he's got to quit the funny business, or it's all over between us. But the man is irrepressible.

On a cold morning he said, "I wish I had a bedpan."

"Do you want me to get your pajama top?"

"My *pajama* top? Oh, you mean the one with the pocket."

I giggle like a ten-year-old. "Chris, you're so ridiculous! I love you!"

"Good. Next time someone asks me, 'What in hell does she see in you?' I'll explain, 'It's because I'm so ridiculous.'"

December 2, 1972
Westwood

Chris would appreciate a wife. Someone to have dinner waiting for him, keep his house neat, do his laundry, darn his socks. *Damn* his socks! I love him too much to let marriage in through the door while courtship slips out the back window. The excitement of seeing each other again after a few days' separation, the shared jokes, the touching—all destroyed by a scrap of paper that would make an honest woman of me? No!

Chris accepts our part-time affair on my terms, albeit ruefully. "Some fellows can settle back occasionally when they're seeing a lady. Others never can."

Not as long as I stay single, they can't. I said to him last night, "Chris, I'll bet we wouldn't make love nearly so often if we were married."

"That's the best reason for not getting married *I* ever heard."

December 10, 1972
Westwood

Ed is courting me more persistently than ever. Knowing nothing about Chris except that there *is* a Chris, he refers to him as "that marshmallow." He admits he's jealous and unhappy. My better self is sorry he is suffering. My baser self isn't. Both selves feel guilty that I am having so much fun. Whenever Chris and I are laughing or making love, a small corner of my psyche is aware of Ed. I wish he could find happiness, too.

I have agreed to go to Fort Lauderdale with him for the holidays.

December 11, 1972
Westwood

Mother invited me to lunch so we could say good-bye before she leaves for Florida. She was waiting for me in her doorway, still radiant and beautiful at seventy-nine.

I talked of nothing but Chris, of course:

"Last night we were holding hands when his daughter called. He talked with her, still hanging on to my hand. Then he needed a pencil for a phone number. Would he part with my hand during this maneuver, even for a minute? No, Mom, he tucked it under his leg, like this, as if telling it, 'Don't go away, I'll be right back.'"

Mom liked Chris's definition of bittersweet: I was talking about a colorful arrangement I'd seen and asked him if he knew what bittersweet was. "Sure I do," he said. "It's that stuff you pick up off the floor after it's dried out."

And his response when I lovingly referred to his soft, caressable arms. "*Soft arms?* Barbara, will you please give me something I can use? How can I tell *that* to the guys at the office?"

Mother is puzzled by my disinterest in marriage but accepts my reasons. "Do whatever is best for you, darling."

I kissed her good-bye and wished her a safe trip.

December 15, 1972
Westwood

I didn't know I would miss her so much. I didn't know how much I still needed her.

Mother died of a heart attack day before yesterday.

Ed called from Detroit and was stunned by my news. "Oh, *no*, not your mother. I loved your mother."

I calmly made the funeral arrangements. Then, last night, the enormity of my loss hit me. My reaction was to turn, not to Chris, but to the comrade I had known for thirty-two years. *PLEASE COME. I NEED YOU.* And I clung to Edward through the long, dark hours, lamenting, lamenting.

December 16, 1972
Westwood

I keep picturing Mother as I last saw her five days ago, waiting for me in her doorway, a welcoming smile lighting her face. Yesterday the funeral director asked me if I wanted to step into the next room where Mother . . . *no*. Mother wasn't in that room, only her "old overcoat," as she once called it.

It took me less than a moment's thought to decline the funeral director's offer. I was certain my mother wouldn't want me to look at the shell that had held her vital, glowing, loving self.

December 27, 1972
Westwood

For the umpteenth time I have read Mother's poem "The Measure" and am struck by how poignantly it applies to her, as well as to the beloved person she had in mind, my father.

> The strong warm hand, the broad and steady shoulder,
> The face you love grown dearer, kinder, older,

The comrade-glance, the peace, the burden-sharing,
The well-loved voice, the touch, the tender caring . . .
O you who have this, guard it well and treasure it,
For only when you've lost it can you measure it!

December 31, 1972
Fort Lauderdale, Florida

To Chris

It is 9:20 P.M. on the last day of 1972. Dick Van Dyke is teetering on a ledge outside his office, Ed has floated off to bed on a cloud of pink champagne, and I am thinking of you. All day I have felt as if I were coming down with something, and now I know what it is . . . a love letter.

Chris, I *love* you! There, now, I feel better already. Still a bit feverish, but better.

Standing on the balcony today, I remembered how I had looked down at the street two years ago, feeling so desolate that it seemed crazy *not* to jump. Now I can lean my arms on the railing, drink in the view of sea and sky, and think how lucky I am to be alive and in love with my Chris.

I never want to lose you, but if the unthinkable should happen, I'll be a better, stronger person than I was before we met. No one can ever take from me the heart-mending knowledge that you love me.

Now I'm going to stop thinking about the unthinkable because I love you and you're never gonna get away.

On our condo bookshelf I found a magazine containing a poem I'd forgotten:

"The Sky Is High"
by Ernestine Cobern Beyer

The sky is far, the sky is high,
But I can reach it with my eye.

Too deep for wading is the brook,
But I can cross it with a look.

You and I are worlds apart,
But I can reach you with my heart!

I wish I could tell Mother that I'm putting her poem in a New Year's Eve letter to my beloved Chris.

January 7, 1973
Westwood

"Notice my missing inches, honey?" I asked Chris in bed, after two weeks of Florida swimming and jogging.

"I'm noticing a lot of things," he murmured. "I'll get to those later."

I asked Chris for a report on the books I gave him to read while I was away. "Tell me how the species originated."

"Well, it's a long story."

He hadn't read *Vietnam Armageddon*, either. "If you'll just read those two chapters, Chris, we'll forget everything else—the Kennedy assassination, Watergate, everything. At least I'll know I'm reaching you *somewhere*."

Before he went home, he said, "Honey, if you ever decide we should see each other only two nights a week . . ."

"Yes . . . ?"

"Would you please make it three?"

I think Chris and I can stay in love forever as long as we don't get married. I'm too enamored of my freedom to settle again into the tender trap of domesticity. Feather-lined or ruby-studded, a trap doesn't provide much living space.

The following letter was written to Massachusetts congressman James Burke, who had called my mother when she went to Washington to accept an award from the

National League of Pen Women. He had a son who wrote poetry; he invited her to meet him for lunch.

January 15, 1973
Westwood

To Congressman James Burke

On April 13, 1972, you gave a talk in the House of Representatives which began, "I feel as though I should share my good fortune in knowing such a wonderful person as Ernestine Cobern Beyer."

I'm sure you will want to know that eight months later, on December 13, my mother passed away. The shock was particularly great to all of us who loved her because we had so little warning. She had been ill a few weeks earlier but appeared to be fully recovered, as pretty and peppy as ever.

You can imagine how much I will miss my precious mother. One thing that makes life without her a little easier to bear is the remembrance of your kindness to her last spring. She had been reluctant to take the trip to Washington, but my husband and I urged her to go. How glad we are that she did, for she came home bubbling with the news of the most wonderful experience of her lifetime.

When she received the copies of the *Congressional Record* containing your tribute, she was overwhelmed. Of course, in her modest way she felt that your praise was far more than she deserved.

Until then, it had troubled me that she had not received more appreciation and recognition for her extraordinary gifts. Your speech provided a long-overdue climax to her life. Everything you had to say about her was exactly right . . . my heart and eyes are filled as I reread your words.

Now that she is gone I expect the world will suddenly discover Ernestine Beyer. I will always be grateful to you that you discovered her first and let her know how much you valued what you found.

May 5, 1973
Westwood

Ed said over the phone, "If Chris and I meet at the golf club opening, I'll shake hands with him, of course. But I'll have a poisoned pin in mine."

I reported this to Chris, who said, "I'll wear gloves."

May 20, 1973
Westwood

I asked Chris what he'd decided about going up to Maine with me. "Tell me how you really feel."

"Tell you how I really feel? Well . . . I love you very much—and if you ever get in trouble I'll marry you."

I told him I had a very good reason for keeping my distance for a few days. "You wouldn't thank me if you caught my poison ivy."

"Yes I would, yes I would!"

June 9, 1973
South Casco, Maine

After a beautiful afternoon of sunning and talking, Chris and I walked toward our cabin. I paused to look at the sun setting over the lake and was sorry my camera was broken.

"What are you standing out there for, lovey?" Chris asked from the doorway.

"I'm just looking, feeling, smelling, enjoying . . ."

"Well, come on in, honey, we can do all that in the cabin."

I told Chris that Ed complains of difficulty in finding com-

"Well, come on in, honey, we can do all that in the cabin."

panionship on the nights he doesn't see me. "He says they're either too young or too ugly or too uninteresting."

"They're too not you, Barbara."

June 20, 1973
Westwood

Our third (fourth ? fifth?) Big Fight.

"They were going to use these call girls on a cruiser to lure Democrats aboard," I told him, "and . . ."

"They were *going* to?"

"If Liddy's plan had been accepted, that's what they were going to do."

"You shouldn't say that, you should say, 'This is what they *would have done*,' not 'what they were going to do.' And who do you mean by 'they'?"

"You're nit-picking again, Chris. I didn't say they'd done it, I said this was what they were going to do *if* the plan had been accepted. Everyone knows the plan wasn't accepted, and everyone knows who 'they' are—those creeps, the Committee to Re-elect the President. It just shows how their shifty minds worked. You'd know these things, too, if you read the front page occasionally."

July 1, 1973
Westwood

I've just finished a Silva Mind Control course in which I learned a dream-programming technique. Before I went to bed last night I asked my subconscious what direction my relationship with Ed should take. I woke at 6:45 and remembered the following dream:

Ed and I were up in our plane, coming in over the ocean for a landing. There was a beach to our right. We seemed to be very low, but I didn't see an airport. I figured we must be on our downwind leg. He should be making a base turn any minute.

Instead of turning, Ed continued to descend toward the water. Suddenly the nose of the airplane lifted upward in a stall attitude so severe that we were almost vertical and would shortly drop like lead to our deaths. I remember asking, Why is he doing this? By then the plane had changed so that we no longer sat side by side; *he was now behind me.* (As I write this, the message hits me and I break into tears.)

Then I felt the plane skid through the water and onto the beach. I asked Ed what went wrong and he said he didn't know.

We went into a hotel where we seemed to have reservations. We walked down a hall toward two doorways. Ed said, "This one must be ours," and opened the door on the right.

To my embarrassment I caught a glimpse of a bed and heard voices protesting this invasion of privacy. As I turned to walk away from the room, a man put his arm around my waist and I in turn embraced him. We walked hurriedly away, laughing and hugging each other. It was as if he wanted to ease my embarrassment. He was a tall man wearing glasses like Chris's.

Ed was left behind.

October 16, 1973
Westwood

To Floyd Rinker

Your enthusiasm for Dubrovnik is contagious. How exciting it would be if my camera and I could join forces with you for a future visit! Do you have a pill or two we could slip Chris to keep him tranquil while we're away?

I have ordered a bigger and better enlarger that I am counting on to produce bigger and better pictures. I will want to do more traveling, once my divorce settlement is final. Ed, whose mood changes from week to week, is currently being kind, friendly, and cooperative. He even asked if I would continue to date him after the divorce.

I have been using Mind Control techniques to conjure up an attractive lady friend for Ed, so he will be happier. I have also been working on the arthritis in your right hand. Is it Better and Better?

I said to Chris the other day, if I were seventy and could return to any age I desired, I would go back no further than fifty. That was when I was born—with your help, Dr. Rinker. . . .

December 17, 1973
Westwood

Chris told me that to this day he still ends his prayers with "God bless me and make me a good boy." "It got to be a habit," he explained. Then he gave me a hug and added, "And now He's made me a good girl."

He told me about a dream *he* had. "You and Ed were traveling around in Sicily. I kept trying to get to see you, but I had to pretend I was just leaving or I wasn't there. All you and Ed ever saw of me was my back. I'd stand outside the place where you were staying, hoping he'd come out so I could go in."

I commented to Chris that Ed can't stand being alone, especially at night. "You're different," I added. "You like watching sports or gardening or refinishing furniture—you enjoy your own company."

"I pretend I'm not there," Chris said.

September 24, 1974
Westwood
To Ed

If you want to see me once a week, I'm willing to give it a try. Twice a week is too much, I can't do justice to either relationship if you keep competing time-wise and sex-wise with Chris. Let me be like one of your old married-to-someone-else women friends you see once in a while. Maybe then it'll be "thrilling and exciting" instead of traumatic.

November 30, 1974
Fort Lauderdale

From Ed

By the time you get this you'll be truly free, or within a few hours of freedom.* I'll never be free no matter what happens. Since you left, I've lived in a world of shadows except for those moments when I've been with you. Certainly, there have been other people and events; but like raindrops running down a window, they happen and they're gone. Always my heart, my love are with you.

I know in my reasoning brain that I've lost you forever; but my dreams, my romantic fantasies keep saying, "This too will pass; she'll come back someday."

Oh, dear God, the time races by, the days are lost, my life is racing by, there just isn't enough time to court you, wait for you, strive for you, love you. Why couldn't all this have happened ten years sooner so that I'd have ten more years to get you back?

Dear heart, love me.

---

*The divorce became final on December 7, 1974.

Eight

My Cherished Ex-Husband
(1981–1986)

Yesterday's christening was at the Unitarian Church, with two pews reserved for Malleys and their in-laws. As the service began, Kaitlin, the four-month-old star of the show, was there in the custody of her parents—our son Ted and his wife, Maureen. Maureen's parents, Papa Joe and Barbara Barry, were in charge of our energetic grandson, two-year-old Teddy, an honor Ed and I didn't begrudge them. Also present were Maureen's sisters and her friend Kelly, plus other assorted relatives and friends.

As a happily ex-married couple, Great White Eagle and I were missing. Ed had agreed that I would drive to his house from Weymouth in my new Chevette; we would then proceed to the church together in his Toyota. I arrived at Ed's just three minutes behind schedule, expecting to find him waiting at the wheel of the Toyota with the motor running. That's where *I'd* be if *he* were three minutes late; but Ed's mind

A good ex-husband is hard to find.

rarely follows the same exquisitely logical course as mine. No
Ed. And no Toyota.

I honked the horn on my Chevette until the button fell off,
a weakness of 1980 Chevettes. Then I banged on Ed's door
and heard barks and thuds on the other side—Miette trying to butt her way out. Next I checked Ted and Maureen's
house; no Ed. So I drove to the church alone. Ed, handsomely
dressed for the occasion, was waiting on the steps, motioning
to me to hurry.

"You said you'd wait—," I scolded as I ran toward him.

"Shh," he said.

"Why are you shushing—," I began, then saw the usher

standing behind Ed, holding the church door open for us. Oh-oh! I was Making a Scene.

"Why didn't you wait?" I whispered as soon as we were seated.

"*Shh,*" Edward said.

"Will the congregation please rise?" said the Reverend Atkinson.

"I'd have waited for you," I whispered.

"You're perfect," Ed whispered back. He sure knows how to hurt a guy.

"What's that man up there talkin' about?" a stentorian voice in the pew behind us inquired. Heads turned to see who it was. I knew without turning: our grandson Teddy.

Now it was time for the christening. Ted and Maureen left their pew, the baby in Maureen's arms.

"I wanna go, too!" caroled Teddy.

Papa Joe explained softly that baby sister was going to be christened.

"I wanna be christened, too!"

"You *had* your turn; now it's Katie's turn."

"After Katie's turn, *Teddy's* turn," announced my grandson, who knows what's fair.

I had a helpful thought. I handed my ballpoint pen, shaped like a golf club, back to Teddy. *That* should keep him occupied for a while.

Teddy gazed at the pen, then proclaimed to the congregation: "*Now I need a golf ball.*"

"*Shh,*" said Papa Joe.

" . . . and I christen thee Kaitlin Barbara Malley."

A thump to my solar plexus. I hadn't known it would sound so soul-warming.

I turned around to see why Teddy had stopped talking. Papa Joe had sealed our grandson's lips with a Band-Aid.

Teddy briskly peeled off the Band-Aid and insisted loudly that it was now *his* turn to be christened. His face flushed with righteous indignation; his voice had an added resonance. He would make a fine preacher. Papa Joe and Teddy departed for a little walk outdoors. I whispered to Ed, "Did you notice how quiet it got after Joe left?"

Ed promptly stole my joke. "Did you notice how quiet it got after Joe left?" he asked Barbara Barry and her daughter Susan. Then he leaned across the aisle and repeated the jest to Ted and Maureen. I remained modestly in the background, wigwagging over his shoulder, "*My* joke, *my* joke."

On the way out, the best thing happened: Teddy kicked Maureen's friend Kelly. I'd been supposing he reserved all his kickings for me.

February 17, 1981
Weymouth

I was stepping out of the tub when I heard my condo buzzer. Chris arriving early. As he came through the large door facing my apartment at the end of the hall, I waved to him from my doorway and called, "I just got out of the shower. I'll be with you in a minute." I left the door ajar so he could walk in while I put on a robe.

Chris: "When you first opened the door, I thought you weren't wearing anything—at least that's the way it looked from the end of the hall."

Me: "Were you wearing your glasses?"

Chris: "Yes, thank God!"

March 20, 1981
Weymouth

Ed has a new doll for his collection—and I discovered her.

In December Marion Marsh invited me to attend a Unitarian social gathering at the home of Robert Rimmer, author of *The Harrad Experiment*. The book created a sensation in 1966; today's youngsters may wonder what the fuss was about. The plot concerned a coed university where students were required to change sexual partners every few months; Rimmer thought this would provide valuable insights when the time came to select a more permanent partner.

We were served wine and cheese and taken on a tour of Rimmer's book-lined house. Dozens of copies of each of his many books filled the shelves. After the tour, I found myself sitting next to Stanley, a balding, pleasant-faced man, chatting about this and that.

I was enjoying the subtle undercurrents a woman senses when a new acquaintance finds her interesting and attractive. As I delivered one of my better quips, however, I noticed that Stanley was no longer tuned in. His gaze was fixed on an area over my right shoulder; the undercurrents had made a treacherous detour.

"Hi, Cleo!" my ex-companion called, leaping to his feet and landing on one of mine.

Was this the Siren of the Nile? Peering around Stanley, who was holding out his arms and puckering up his lips, I looked her over. Cleo was tallish, blondish, fiftyish, and hadn't given up the fight yet; I could tell by her figure and false eyelashes. I leaned toward Marion and whispered, "Who's that?"

"That? Stanley Nesbitt."

"No, no, that woman he's fawning over. Is she married?" Marion said she'd seen Cleo in church, didn't know her last name, thought she might be getting a divorce.

"I hope so," I said. "She's Edward's type if I ever saw Edward's type. He's never been able to resist a pair of false eyelashes—and he's shopping around."

Marion thinks I'm crazy. She keeps asking when Ed and I are going to quit kidding and get married again. She pooh-poohs my arguments that his house is too hot, his TV too loud, and his poodle too undisciplined. Marion is sure that for my sake Edward would turn down the heat and TV and spank the poodle. But it wouldn't work. It exhausts me even to think of my weekly treks, watering can in hand, through the burgeoning jungle he has created, like some mad botanical Frankenstein, in his living room. Watering his plants takes more time than I have left. Let Cleo do it.

I liked the way she was bantering with Stanley. Any woman who waters Edward's plants *must* have a sense of humor.

Two weeks later I bumped into Cleo standing with a plump friend in front of the perfume counter at Jordan's. I sidled up and muttered in her ear, "Personally, I wouldn't care for all that partner swapping in *The Harrad Experiment*, would you?"

She looked at me blankly for a moment, then grinned and said, "I stick to swapping recipes."

We stepped away from the counter and small-talked. Then I plunged in and told her about Ed. I must have painted a glowing portrait because Cleo's plump friend swung around and asked, "How old is he?" "Sixty-five." She went back to her perfume sniffing as if I'd said ninety-nine. No problem; he wouldn't be interested in her, either.

Cleo wasn't so negative. "Any ex-husband of yours must be a nice guy. Why don't you bring Ed to the church next Sunday afternoon? They're having a get-together for singles."

Ed was seeing Aliceann Sunday night, but he said sure, he'd go to the singles thing with me in the afternoon. What did he have to lose?

"I'll pretend you're my brother," I told Ed. "Otherwise people will wonder why we have the same last name." We signed in at the door, stuck on our name tags, and drifted over to the wine and cheese table. I nudged Ed. "She's over there—in the red dress."

Edward stared for a moment, then asked, "How do I get to meet her?"

I promptly introduced them. Cleo linked her arm in Ed's, gave him a flutter with those eyelashes, and that was that: mission accomplished.

They've seen each other several times since then, but Ed is in a quandary. He doesn't know what to do about Aliceann. He asked her to marry him a few months ago, with my enthusiastic approval; but when she learned pets weren't allowed in his Florida condo, she said no. Then she heard he's seeing someone else and called *me* to ask *my* advice. Refusing to marry him didn't mean she was ready to give him up. She said she didn't know who this other woman was, but she was just going to hang in there, didn't I agree that was what she should do? I felt crumby because I really like Aliceann; but Ed comes first in my list of priorities. If only everyone could find exactly the right partner. Maybe the solution would be for me to find someone for Aliceann.

April 30, 1981
Weymouth

Ed and I just got back from our longest stay yet in Florida, almost four weeks. We drove to Key West to see Ted and his family; then Ted came back to Fort Lauderdale with us for a couple of days of golf.

I asked Ted if he'd heard about the new woman in his father's life.

"A couple of rumors, that's all."

Ed's ears turned pink. When they didn't deepen to red, I decided it was safe to tell Ted the whole Siren of the Nile saga.

"What a soap opera!" Ted commented. "What characters! What twists of plot! You can be the leading lady."

The Leading Lady . . . I like it, I like it!

July 24, 1981
Weymouth

At first I was pleased when last spring's matchmaking worked out so well. Cleo thought Ed was a "dear man," and Ed thought Cleo was not only attractive but sympathetic and undemanding. ("She never asks who else I'm seeing or what I'm doing when I'm not with her.") As time went by he began reshuffling his social calendar to see more of Cleo.

Then I began to notice he was seeing less of me. He was no longer my dependable golfing buddy; instead, he and Cleo were going on picnics or planting rosebushes. A couple of times even our Thursday night dinner date was called off for one vague reason or another. Once, he said he'd see me Friday night instead, then begged off with the excuse that he was too tired. What could be making that man so tired? Of course, all I have ever wanted with all my heart and soul was for Ed to be happy.

But not *that* happy.

I didn't complain openly. I did a lot of empathizing with Aliceann, though. Following her example, I decided I'd hang in there. Ex-husbands like Ed are hard to find.

He hasn't abandoned me entirely. He invited me to join Cleo and him for dinner at the golf club Wednesday night. His rationale? "I want her to get used to you." I said no. She'll have to get used to me soon enough without my encroaching on their dates.

Meanwhile, Ed, Aliceann, and I are still a threesome, attending doll auctions and antique shows together. The Pied Piper of Scituate is doing his best to keep everyone contented, as well as in line. He seems a bit dazed by it all.

July 28, 1981
Weymouth

Claire Swann is another complication. Claire was Ed's steady companion a couple of years ago. Then she drifted into the arms and Beacon Hill apartment of a man I'll call G.P., because that's what the tabloids called him in headlines from coast to coast. Claire's ex-husband filed a sort of reverse palimony suit, claiming she had violated a clause in their divorce contract. She had agreed not to live with a man, "giving the appearance of marriage." Since she was living with Mr. G.P., her ex-husband sued to retrieve thousands of dollars in alimony he alleged she had collected unlawfully.

The case went to court, and soon the papers were splashing their front pages with G.P. headlines. Claire's defense: she had never passed herself off as Mrs. G.P.; she paid her share of their living expenses, including those incurred when she and G.P. traveled together. Moreover, she continued to date other men, including a certain Mr. E.M.

I took a ribbing at the golf club over the mysterious Mr. E.M. That's one of the things I like about being an ex-wife; you're always the first to know. I assured my friends I had always liked Claire and was rooting for her to win her countersuit.

I was sitting by Ed's pool yesterday when the mailman arrived. Among the letters was an envelope addressed in block letters to "Mr. E.M."

Ed asked, "Who do you suppose sent this?"

"I refuse to guess," I said.

He opened the envelope and read the message: "To someone delectable . . . from someone who knows." Then he threw me a grin. It was signed "Mrs. E.M."

August 22, 1981
Weymouth

Over dinner at Ye Olde Mill Grille, Chris commented that it was good we were going to the 9 : 30 showing of *Eye of the Needle* because "there'll be less people."

"Fewer," I said.

"What?"

"*Fewer* people."

Chris saluted and said, "You've been reading Strunk and White again."

I was wrung out by the end of the movie. As the camera panned over the bleak scene, the lonely island house with cliffs plunging to the beach below, Chris asked, "Doesn't that remind you of the fifteenth hole at Pebble Beach?"

What I will miss most about Chris if we break up forever (again): his gift for generating humor out of nothing, the way a magician plucks colored scarves from the air. How can I split from a man who has kept me laughing for nine years?

Chris has one failing: He shows little interest in good food and the ritual of sharing it. Yet, if he were to develop an appetite and a paunch, *that* would turn me off even more. His tall, slim body is the perfect counterpart for mine. He is so huggable that I can hardly keep my arms to myself even when we're strolling through a supermarket. The younger generation doesn't guess that we older folks still breathe hard on occasion, and not just from climbing stairs.

November 12, 1981
Weymouth

To my sister, Janeth

I feel silly telling you my latest "news," since you've heard it so many times in the last nine years. What I have, I've decided, is a chronic affliction called "Split-with-Chris-itis." I wrote to him the day after we broke up, clarifying what it was all about, since his version of our rows generally turns out to be quite different from mine.

I reminded him that we were both in good spirits when we left my apartment to go out to dinner. We walked down the hall, talking about Ed's friend Aliceann, what a delightful lady she was, how much we liked her, etc. As he opened the lobby door, he looked down at me and said, "And I'll bet she'd never be a soreass."

We both knew that "soreass" was his latest pet name for me. It didn't charm me as much as "angel" used to, but he had a way of saying it that made me laugh—the first couple of times, that is. This time I could see no humor in the remark. In my letter I said it was too bad he couldn't be complimentary to Aliceann without putting me down. At the top of the first page I wrote, "Go ahead and tear this up without reading it—but don't call me because I'll hang up."

This happened three weeks ago. I haven't heard from my erstwhile Sweet Prince, so I haven't had a chance to hang up. What stubborn, unreasonable beasts men can be.

November 18, 1981
Weymouth

Chris called yesterday after a month's silence, wanting to know if I was still mad. His explanation for his "soreass" remark was that *I* was the furthest thing from his mind when he said it; he was thinking of Ed's other friend, Patty. Why had it taken him so long to come up with this story? Because he was mad at the things I said when *I* was mad. He'll probably work his way back into my good graces, but if I ever hear the word "soreass" again, he'd better run for cover.

February 28, 1982
Weymouth

Cleo has ended her relationship with Ed. She felt she was standing in the way of his finding someone he could settle down with permanently. Ed wants either marriage or a live-in mate; Cleo wants neither. I advised Ed to marry Aliceann. He said, "Don't lobby me; lobby her."

May 16, 1982
Weymouth

Me to Chris: I'm glad your prostate surgery doesn't interfere with your sex life. I'll bet a lot of men would be affected out of sheer panic.
Chris: Not me. I'm not going to give this up, no matter *what* they take out!

May 22, 1982
Weymouth

Ed has sold his last plane, but not before I had a chance to show Chris how well I can fly it. His friends at the bank were incredulous when he told them his lady had flown him to Martha's Vineyard—and back, too. I was also incredulous. Ed has left me with many warm memories; our mutual love affair with flying is one of the richest.

We still share the Florida condominium every spring. Our compatibility is the kind that develops when you "grow up" together.

Chris's buddies were next mystified by the news that his lady was in Fort Lauderdale with her ex-husband. People have a hard time figuring us out. Luckily, we don't have to defer to "what people think."

Chris is retiring in June, the day before our tenth anniversary. Ed will have his new boat in the water by then, so we can look forward to fishing and picnicking. Perhaps one or both of them will fall overboard so I'll have something to write about.

July 17, 1982
Weymouth

Last Sunday's outing didn't provide enough action for a boating article, but it wasn't a total loss. Ed brought Aliceann along with her usual hamper of goodies.

After an hour at sea Ed and I agreed we should have made an earlier start. We decided to end up at Plymouth instead of Provincetown. He left me at the wheel with instructions to "keep her on the course she's on now."

When Captain Ed Boatguy next showed up, we were nearing the "dip in the land" he had pointed out. A red nun buoy rode a few hundred yards ahead on our right. Ed took over and I was just sitting down in a deck chair when I was thrown with a lurch to starboard. A prolonged grinding noise— *screech, scruunch*—accompanied the lurch, along with some curses from the flying bridge. Chris, Aliceann, and I looked at each other wide-eyed. Should we prepare to abandon ship?

Our captain, rather the worse for wear, studied the chart again and figured out where the ship had hit the fan, so to speak. What he thought was the number 4 red nun off Plymouth Harbor was actually the number 4 red nun off Green Harbor.

"You managed to find the only rock within a thousand miles," Ed said. "No, she's not leaking, I checked."

We dropped anchor in Scituate Harbor to rest our nerves, and broke out the beer and Aliceann's picnic. What a lovely way to spend a steamy Sunday afternoon! When we were ready to leave, Ed and Chris couldn't free the anchor from whatever it was caught on, no matter how hard they tugged.

"There goes another hundred dollars," Ed grumbled, cutting loose the anchor and chain.

We ended up at Ed's house, dunking ourselves in his pool and sending out for subs and pizza.

September 16, 1982
Weymouth

Ed has put his Scituate house on the market. I'd rather he didn't, but I can't argue with his reasons. He wants to buy a canal-front house in Florida where he can have his boat, his dog, and no more cold winters. Scituate realtors picked up the scent and came swarming in, eager for an exclusive. The first thing they said, in a shocked chorus, was: "Mr. Malley, those plants have got to go!"

The living room jungle had by then exploded into a veritable rain forest. Although Ed ignored the pleas of ex-wives and lady friends, the realtors got to him. Once he understood that his view-blocking vegetation might also block a sale, he manfully set his jaw and invaded his jungle with a hatchet. Two days later he emerged. I had forgotten how beautiful the marsh grass and the river look from Ed's picture windows.

At the Barrys' beach, where our daughter-in-law Maureen's folks have a summer cottage, Maureen and I and her mother and various aunts and cousins sit around deciding what Ed should and should not do. We call our beach-chair group the Ed Malley Management Team. I am the president. The current consensus is that he should rent the Scituate house rather than sell it, then rent a house in Florida to see if he's going to like living down there seven months out of twelve. He wants to sell our Fort Lauderdale condominium, too, of course. I asked him where he's going to live the other five months of the year. "Why, with you, didn't I mention it?"

Ed says he is now broke. He explains he made more money last year than he expected and therefore owes the government more taxes than he set aside. If he'd made less money, would he then be less broke? 'Tis a puzzlement.

February 6, 1983
Fort Lauderdale, Florida

Ed and I are having a fascinating (to me), frustrating (to him) time looking at houses. If it has a dock, deep water, and a garage to putter in, he'd buy it tomorrow. My priorities are a fence or shrubbery for privacy, a pool for Kathie, a large third bedroom for Kathie, Dick, Sarah, and others who may visit, a wide canal, a quiet street, a kitchen with a water view.

We were talking last night about Ed's romance last spring with a woman named Sheila.

"I was never serious about her," he insisted.

"Then how come you invited her to Scituate for a trial engagement?"

"I just wanted her to find out for herself what a mistake she'd be making."

"Edward, I never realized how truly noble and self-sacrificing you are."

"I'm a marvelous person!" he crowed.

I'll be here until the first week in April. This is the longest "same time next year" visit we have had. Ed is full of optimism about living in Florida and hopes that I will become as enamored as he is. It will be an interesting test of togetherness.

February 10, 1983
Fort Lauderdale

Ed and I have been having an ex-marital problem. I want to go to Disney World and Epcot; he doesn't. He has been supportive of *my* going, offering help in making arrangements, but would he go with me? Even for only two nights? All my pleas, arguments, and threats (that I wouldn't come down again if he was going to be so mean) were to no avail.

Then I thought of an arm twister. I remembered he had promised Aliceann he would travel with her if she'd marry him.

"I'm gonna tell," I said. "How can Aliceann believe you'll travel with her, when you won't even take a tiny little three-day trip with your ex-wife!"

Ed capitulated gracefully. "I'll go to Epcot with you, and I'll even have a good time."

Whew! That's the closest I've come to divorcing him again!

February 18, 1983
Fort Lauderdale

There can't be many women who kiss their ex-husbands good-bye and wish them luck with a blind date. Alas, this one was an unmitigated disaster. The lady looked much older than the fifty-seven years she had owned to. Never again, Ed decided, would he answer one of those Personals ads.

March 12, 1983
Weymouth

To Darrell McClure

Ed's life resembles a comic opera. A couple of weeks ago he set out in his old Ford station wagon to pick up Claire at the railroad station in Quincy. So I won't mix up the characters—they can do that very nicely for themselves—I must explain that Claire is the one with the long blonde hair and Southern accent who used to be Ed's regular date but currently sees him only once a week. Aliceann has long black hair crowning her head like a turban, dramatic spectacles, chunky jewelry, a shaggy dog, and an inscrutable cat named Sybil. She is a favored stand-in for Patty of the long, very *very* blonde hair. (I believe there's a contest going on between Patty and Claire to see whose hair can be the most dazzling. If they were together, which is unlikely, a bystander would need sunglasses.)

En route to Quincy, Ed's Ford began to gasp and falter. Mellow as Ed has become in the autumn of his years, I imagine he swore a bit as he made a U-turn and headed for Aliceann's, hoping to borrow his Toyota from her. She was using it because *her* car was in the repair shop. This may be the reason he hangs on to the venerable station wagon; with four ladies in his life, including the one named Barbara with the silky, naturally brown hair, one of us is bound to be having car trouble. We all *do* appreciate Ed's spare wheels.

Aliceann and Ed's Toyota were not at home, so he drove on to Patty's, coaxing a few more miles out of the ailing Ford.

"Why should I lend you *my* car so you can pick *her* up?" Patty demanded. But she surrendered, as Ed's ladies usually do, and off he sped to Quincy, where Claire was tapping her foot in front of the station. End of Scene 1.

In Scene 2, Ed and Claire drive to Aliceann's and find that she has returned from her errand. Claire gets out of Patty's Dodge, climbs into Ed's Toyota, and follows him to Patty's house, where he drops off her Dodge and picks up his Ford. With Claire still following in the Toyota, the wheezing Ford manages to make it to Ed's driveway. End of comic opera.

Ted asked me recently which of Ed's ladies I like best. "I love them all," I said. Actually, Aliceann has an edge because she has a warm, enthusiastic personality and the world's greatest cheesecake recipe. I have some superb recipes, too, but they sit in the cupboard with the instant puddings. Aliceann *uses* hers. She leaves so many treats in Ed's refrigerator he can't keep up with them, so Chris and I help out. Any ex-wife would say the same thing I did when I first sampled Aliceann's apple strudel: "Ed, you've gotta keep this treasure in the family!"

Ed does his best to keep us *all* in the family. Claire, the Wednesday night lady, has a steady named Gerald she sees on weekends. Ed is jealous but reasons that one-seventh of Claire is better than no Claire at all. Weekends, he divides his time between Patty and Aliceann, each of whom is jealous of the other. Patty is several years younger than Aliceann, who always refers to her as Pattycakes— "just to annoy Ed," she confided to me on the way home from the airport. I had driven there to pick her up after her week's vacation with Ed in Fort Lauderdale. (He's staying on alone for a few days.) I don't know what Patty calls Aliceann.

"Is Patty watering your plants the way she promised?" I asked Ed on the phone.

"I don't know; she's pretty mad."

As much as I like Patty, I do think she's being unreasonable. Hadn't she assured Ed from the beginning that it was okay with her, she was dating other men, he was a free agent, etc.? If she's too irked to water the few plants Ed still has left, I suppose I'll have to do it. Might as well be gracious about it; my clutch has been acting funny lately.

Darrell, it's like old times, writing to my favorite correspondent. Happy springtime!

July 11, 1983
Weymounth

To Darrell

No, I haven't thought of a title for the Malley soap opera, but it is still sudsing along in good style. At this point Ed is annoyed with Aliceann because she's annoyed with him because of Patty. She has scarcely spoken to him for a week. The Last of the Red Hot Lovers is getting restless.

"You know how you could save me from marrying any of them?" Ed asked me cagily. "*You* marry me!"

"But what about Chris?" I asked, shocked. "He's practically your best friend! You wouldn't steal his girl away, would you?"

"*Penis erectus non conscientious est*," quoth Ed. (All's fair in love and war.)

Ed didn't need to steal me away. Chris and I had always had our highs and lows, and we frequently broke up "forever." The day came, though, when it was forever.

October 6, 1983
Weymouth

To Chris

After much heart-searching I've come to the conclusion that this reconciliation isn't going to work out. I no longer feel like half of a loving twosome but more like the partner in a not very successful marriage.

It was physical attraction and your adorable sense of humor that kept us going for so many years, despite our bickering over anything and everything. In almost every area of life we perceive things too differently to achieve any real degree of compatibility.

Now that you're retired and thinking of warmer climes, it wouldn't be fair to let you assume I would be in the picture, even on a limited basis, wherever you settle down. I don't see myself anywhere but here on the South Shore, living the single existence I have learned to enjoy.

I assure you I am grateful for the many thoughtful things you have done for me and will always, as you suggested in a recent letter, accentuate the positive memories. I'd have missed a lot if I had never met you.

Chris responded graciously to my letter, and although he moved to California to be near his daughter and grandson, he maintained his friendship not only with me but with Ed and Aliceann.

December 20, 1983
Cedar Grove, California

From Chris

I miss you and think of you very often. You're a tiger and difficult to forget, so I won't.

I see Sharon about every two months, either here or there. Her husband's a great guy and my grandson's terrific.

If I ask you questions, will you answer me? like—are you well and happy and loved by someone new? I hope you are because you have a lot to offer the right man.

Please convey my best wishes to Ed, Aliceann, or whoever you feel would care.

Merry Christmas

December 30, 1983
Weymouth

Ed called yesterday from Fort Lauderdale:

"Why don't you marry me? We could live down here in the winter and up there in the summer, we could play a lot of golf, we'll travel and go on cruises the way you always wanted to—and I'll even go on paying your alimony."

May 13, 1984
Weymouth

Patty's fiancé moved in with her a couple of months ago. We heard that they plan to marry in June and move to his house in Rhode Island. Ed is heartbroken. I keep telling him to be patient. This storybook romance is too good to be true; sooner or later Patty will become available again and Ed will have a second chance.

For Ed, love is either feast or famine. Without Patty in his life, and without much of Claire, my poor ex has found himself reduced from four women to one: Aliceann. I don't count at the moment. I am merely his confidante, the friend who listens to his troubles and watches *Barney Miller* with him once a week.

Ed admits he had a problem with Patty. This tall, slim blonde had a habit of bounding naked into his kitchen while he was making cocktails and exclaiming, "Let's get it on!"

"That kind of approach might have been great twenty years ago," Ed tells me, "but at my age I need a little advance notice. No more quickies; I like slowies."

Aliceann works all week and is often busy weekends, too. Ed is becoming increasingly lonesome and depressed. He has a bum knee that may require surgery; he is fretting over an unresolved business deal; and his love life stinks. No wonder the Sheik of Scituate is restless.

Worried about him, I asked him why he didn't try his luck at the singles cocktail lounge where Pattycakes met her Dreamboat.

"For every woman there," he explained, "there are at least twenty males vying for her attention. How can a man in his sixties cope with all that competition?"

I feel sure there are women out there somewhere—attractive women, lonely women, too shy to go to dating bars. That gave me an inspiration. Why not put an ad in the real estate section of the local paper, offering Ed's apartment at a very low rent in exchange for a house sitter and plant waterer when he's away—and part-time companionship when he isn't? If the ad were tastefully worded, someone passable might turn up.

Ed said he wanted nothing to do with this project, so I called the *Patriot Ledger*'s classified-ads department myself. I had some difficulty with the woman to whom I dictated my script. I wanted it to read: "*Fantastic Opportunity*—Semi-retired bachelor with beautiful waterfront South Shore home offers adjoining efficiency apt. with separate entrance. Incredibly low rent in exchange for light housekeeping one day a week & assistance with occasional formal dinner parties. If you are a cultured woman 45–55, trim & attractive, write *Patriot Ledger* Box ——."

Right off the bat, I was informed that I couldn't use the word "bachelor." I changed it to "executive." The ad taker doubted that the word "woman" could be used, and I *certainly* couldn't specify that she be trim and attractive. That would sound too much like one of those Personals ads and could get the *Ledger* into trouble. I stuck to my guns on gender, pointing out that my "boss" wasn't looking for a Japanese houseboy. After a conference with higher-ups, my adversary allowed "woman" and "cultured" to stay in the ad.

Ed read the replies but refused to interview anyone. He said he was through hurting people by rejecting them.

I said okay, *I'd* phone the letter writers and interview them. "I'll tell them you're out of town, and I'm your sister-in-law," I added. I had a feeling no woman would enjoy being inspected by an ex-wife.

"I'm laying down taking a nap," twanged my first callee. "Tell your brother-in-law to call me when he gets back." The hell I will, I said to myself.

I interviewed a chain-smoker named Bernice with a fifteen-year-old daughter; she decided the apartment wasn't big enough for their combined life-styles. Good. I didn't like her, anyway.

Olga was an overweight matron of forty-nine. She was eager to move right in and wondered if my brother-in-law would object to her German shepherd; she'd have to keep him chained in the yard while she was at work. Scratch Olga. Scratch the dog.

Rachel had told me over the phone that she was younger than the ad specified, but she was *very* interested and would like to see the apartment. I told her I'd meet her at Ed's at

6:30 on Wednesday. (During these interviews, Ed usually hid in Ted's house next door.)

"Hmm, *now* we're getting somewhere!" I thought when I opened the front door for Rachel, a tall, very pretty brunette. She *loved* the apartment, *loved* the water view, and was sure she'd get along with Mr. Malley, whose picture I had shown her. She was known, she added, for having a way with older folks. I flinched. "How old are *you?*" I asked, sensing that this conversation was taking a turn Ed wouldn't relish if he could hear it.

"Twenty-six."

Too bad. I'd been on the point of calling Ed to hurry home and meet Rachel.

"You're just the type he's looking for," I assured Rachel, "but I know he wants someone nearer his own age."

"I guess he doesn't want a housekeeper as much as a sort of hostess-companion, is that the idea?"

"You've got it." Then on a wild chance I added, "If you know or meet anyone who might fill the bill, have her call me."

The next day Rachel's co-worker, Doris, phoned. Rachel had shown her the ad and she was interested. "I think I'm the sort of person your brother-in-law has in mind."

Doris was a winner; she reminded me of my niece, Linda. Not just the brown eyes or the shoulder-length auburn hair. Something about the shape of her face. Doris had parents in Michigan. Did I think Mr. Malley would mind if they visited her once or twice a year?

"No, I'm sure he wouldn't; but I think you should discuss all these practical things with him personally."

I called Ted's house. Ed wasn't there. Where the devil was he?

"I know. He's probably on his way home from the golf club. He's very bashful. If he sees a strange car in the driveway, he may drive off again. So let's get into *your* car and see if we can find him."

Sure enough, we passed Ed sneaking along within a block or two. By the time we had turned around and reached the driveway, bashful Ed was stomping away from the side door of the house, scowling and muttering profanities; it was locked. Oh, dear, I *had* wanted him to make a good first impression.

"The front door's open," I called sweetly, hoping to soothe the savage beast.

Ed caught sight of Doris and did a double take. I introduced them, then scrammed over to Ted's, leaving the prospective landlord and his prospective tenant to discuss practicalities.

Ed invited Doris in for a drink. He forgot to discuss practicalities, such as how much the incredibly low rent would be. Later, he patted me on the back for my good taste and said Doris was going to give him her decision next week.

Early Saturday morning my phone rang.

"Guess what's happened now," said Ed.

"Claire broke up with Gerald?"

"No, Patty broke up with Whatsisname. What do I do now? Her friend Brenda tells me she's thrown him out of the house."

"Hmmm," I said.

"I thought I wanted Patty more than anything else in the world, but I'm kind of intrigued with the idea of Doris moving in, and the more I think of those teenage kids of Patty's—"

"Now wait a minute, Ed, just because she's thrown Whatsisname out doesn't mean she's going to fall into your lap. Remember all the times I broke up with Chris and how often we made up? I'll bet Patty and Whatsisname will get back together again."

"You're right, I'll just sit tight and see what happens."

Last night I noticed a bouquet in Ed's refrigerator. Ed ex-

*Aliceann has a warm, enthusiastic personality and the
world's greatest cheesecake recipe.*

plained he had bought the flowers to take to Patty. She had
come to the door, her face still swollen from crying.

"She looked miserable! But before I had a chance to com-
miserate with her, she told me her friend had moved in again."

That's why the flowers are in the refrigerator. He's going to give them to Doris. Tomorrow night he's taking her to a champagne reception at the Museum of Fine Arts. I hope he gets around to discussing practicalities, like two hundred dollars a month plus utilities.

February 14, 1986
Weymouth

Surprise! The Ed Malley Management Team has a new president. Ed and Aliceann were married this morning in Ed's new Pompano Beach house. Pets allowed. The ceremony was witnessed by a few local friends plus Miette, Strumpfe, Sybil, and a new Siamese kitten, Ling-Ling.

I phoned them both my blessings; but I told Aliceann I'll miss Ed after all these years.

"Nonsense," she told me. "You're *family*. If you don't promise to visit us, we're gonna *divorce* you."

Nine

Last Word
(1986–1988)

*How did I really feel after surrendering the presidency
of the Ed Malley Management Team? And what happened next?*
    Quite a lot, as a matter of fact.

February 28, 1986
Weymouth, Massachusetts
To my sister, Janeth

Ed has been married for two weeks now, and we seem to be
surviving our final severance without too much loss of blood.
Aliceann is still the same good friend she was before February 14. She assures me that "this is your house, too," and
urges me to come for a visit. I will not do so until the marriage is older and unquestionably on solid ground.

The honeymooners call me every three or four days to exchange news. A couple of nights ago Aliceann was on the line
when I heard a burst of Ed's laughter in the background. "Oh,

The Ed Malley Management Team: Aliceann, Ed, Barbara.

Barbara, you should see what's happening," Aliceann said. "Strumpfe was trying to hump Miette, and she got mad and chased him off the bed."

What did I feel besides amusement? A pang. Worse than a hangnail, not as bad as a toothache, but a definite pang. Ed's laughter was now Aliceann's instead of mine, I thought. Yet I knew this was foolish—you can't own laughter any more than you can own people. And haven't I been insisting that all I want for Ed is his happiness? In the right-thinking part of my mind, my feeling was one of gratitude that Aliceann was *there* for him to laugh with.

The pang is subsiding. Transferring it to paper is helpful, as always.

My own life is far from withering on the vine. Now that Chris and I have parted for good, I find my women friends are as much fun as men and seldom cause pangs or pain. Lucille and I were trying to analyze why our perspective has changed so radically. In our younger days, we decided, we were always competing with other women, inclined to see them as rivals and wary, therefore, of genuine closeness. I'm glad that nonsense is behind me. The cynic who said "Screw the Golden Years" must be a youngster of fifty.

Lucille is the catalyst of our group. She is outrageous, irreverent, generous to a fault, and politically perfect like me. Another lively friend in our Oriental brush class is Cathy. When the three of us were driving to a restaurant recently, Cathy related the following vignette about her marriage:

"When I was forty-two I thought I was pregnant. That night my husband and I were sitting up in bed, reading. I said, 'I think I'm pregnant. If I am, I'll kill myself.' Irving stared at me for a moment, then said, 'I'll help you.'"

When I mentioned that I was going to have an operation on my breast in March, Cathy exclaimed, "Why didn't you tell me this sooner so I could start worrying about you? I'm an Olympic champion worrier, you know."

"It's just a nodule; the doctor says not to lose any sleep over it. Besides, how can I complain when my friends have all overcome more serious problems? Sylvia lost both breasts, June a kidney, Lucille a lung, Cathy her uterus."

"There isn't a complete person in the whole art class!" Lucille chortled.

Then we had a marvelous idea. We decided the three of us should troop down to Florida and have our faces lifted. A Pygmalion, that's what we needed.

"We'll stay at Ed's, and Aliceann will take care of us," I said.

"And wash our bandages," said Lucille.

"And Ed can pay the bills," Cathy added in her practical way.

The hilarity was such that I don't know how Cathy was able to concentrate on her driving. Lucille and I were both gasping.

"Lucille," I wheezed, "I don't know how you can laugh so hard with only one lung!"

"What did you say? *Only one lung?*" Lucille whooped. It's a good thing we had our seat belts on or we'd have been on the floor. My face hurt. I told my friends I would have to stop seeing them; I could feel my skin developing permanent puckers.

Deep down, I know they're worth it. And besides, there's always Dr. Pygmalion.

May 31, 1986
Weymouth

To Ed and Aliceann Malley

My pal Lucille has a new kitten, fluffy white, which she has named Powderpuff. There are four other cats in the Nelson household, plus Rascal, a golden retriever with a beautiful smile and a habit of nudging visitors in the crotch. I was never sure how to respond to this approach until Lucille told me her neighbor's reaction—"*Thank* you!" When Powderpuff isn't bouncing around the house or rubbing noses with the other animals, who find her fascinating, she is stretched out next to the master.

"I didn't know how Harry would feel about another cat," Lucille said, "but he fell for her right away. She lies on her back next to him, her tummy arched and her legs spread out like a whore. How could he resist?"

Radiation news: No side effects so far, except that I have a fantastic single-breasted tan, and the radiated boom-boom is twice as big as the other boom. I am told this effect might be permanent. Hmm, what do I do then—see a plastic surgeon about adding an inch or two to the boom? Or hope to find exactly the right man, a type who likes variety but is rather lazy. Whenever he felt like roving, he could just switch sides.

Time to leave, dears, the sunshine on my balcony says so.

July 26, 1986
Weymouth

To Aliceann

I thought taking pictures of your handmade paper dolls would be a simple assignment—surely easier than photographing people. Not on a breezy Saturday, it isn't. People don't blow away, paper dolls do. I hadn't even taken Miss Lady Golfer out of her plastic page when off she flew while I was busy adjusting my camera. I went scrambling after the cartwheeling page, then had to chase the black cloth I had put on the ground as a backdrop. I hoped my Weymouthport neighbors were all at the pool and not looking out their windows at the old broad's peculiar antics.

I sought out a more sheltered spot by the stairway next to the barbecue area. I placed Miss L.G. on the black cloth, moving her and her outfits around until I was satisfied with the composition. I poised myself to snap the shutter—but wait. Whose shadow is intruding on my subject? Oh . . . mine. I moved my head this way and that, but short of cutting it off, could not get rid of the shadow.

I needed my head to think with. How about going to the opposite side of the display and taking the pictures upside down? Aha, no shadow. Clever Barbara. Will Aliceann be clever enough to turn them right side up again? I'm sure she will.

A young man approached the stairway and asked (rather cautiously, I thought) what I was doing.

"Cutting out—I mean, taking pictures of paper dolls," I said. At that moment Miss L.G.'s golfing outfit took off, followed by its matching straw hat. "As you can see, it isn't easy," I added, lunging for the hat, which was trying to hide under a carpet of dropped leaves. It's a good thing you put a black band on that hat, Aliceann, or I never would have spotted it. I could see the dress lying in a corner behind some shrubs and evergreens. Well, it could wait, it wasn't every day I had a chance to talk with a nice young man. Oh, he's gone. Too bad, he missed his chance to hear all about the fascinating hobby of antique-doll collecting from a fascinating older (and older) woman.

I got down on all fours and crawled through briars and branches toward the spot where the golfing dress had flown. If anyone else came along and asked what I was doing, the answer would be hard to believe. "You're looking for an antique paper doll's golfing outfit? Well, well—and there isn't even a full moon."

I wonder if I'll have as much excitement when I use up the rest of the film.

I'm sitting on my balcony writing this letter, which I'll type later. My TV is on loud enough for me to hear the golf and sort of see it through the screen door. Davis Love III is as good-looking as his name. Maybe someday I'll be watching my grandson on the circuit. I played with him and his father yesterday. Every once in a while Teddy would wind up his baseball swing and whack the ball across a brook as if he didn't know it was there. Probably didn't.

I played nine holes with Big Ted before Teddy joined us. He was having a lot of trouble with his game. "Fortunately," he drawled, as only Ted can drawl, "it doesn't matter. I just don't care anymore." Two holes later his ball landed in a trap instead of on the green. I heard some oaths I never taught that boy. I didn't say anything, though. Any son nice enough to invite his mother to play golf can swear all he wants to.

Aliceann, your contribution to Ed's model railroad was so typically thoughtful and generous. Did he ever tell you his first wife used to just groan when she saw all that paraphernalia? I've told everyone how you took him by surprise with your gifts, and they all say he's landed in a bed of roses.

September 13, 1986
Weymouth

To Chris

Since I last wrote my California pen pal, I bought an electric treadmill, fell and burned my knee when I tried to look at my watch (for a moment I envisioned myself sliding along the belt and coming out a lot thinner than when I started), got cancer, had a lumpectomy, started radiation, finished orthodontia, signed a publishing contract with Good Apple, finished radiation, started golfing midseason, and wondered what was going on with you.

Remember the lump you discovered that turned out to be benign? This one wasn't. I'm lucky, though, to live in an era when doctors aren't so quick to throw out the breast with the biopsy. They remove your lymph nodes, and if they're okay you are spared chemotherapy and need only thirty-five days of radiation. I had no side effects except for irritation over the daily drive to Mass. General. I could have written you volumes about my operation, Chris. No, it's too late now, I'm not going to tell you now no matter how much you beg.

I'll tell you this, the greeting card business thrived on the South Shore this spring. Three of us in Ellee's Oriental brush class had operations, one after another. On August 15 we were going to have a big party at the Hingham Yacht Club to celebrate our recoveries, but Cathy, our hostess, got a sore throat that wouldn't go away. She asked her doctor if it could be cancer, and he said, "I don't know." That's what lawsuits have done to diplomacy, I guess. After nearly dying of fright, Cathy got better.

Another good friend is Lucille Nelson. She's the type you like, Chris, a zany madcap with a racy Irish wit. She hasn't the slightest awe of people in authority and expresses herself with uninhibited zest. Before she checked into Quincy Hospital, a Vietnamese anesthesiologist gave her a pre-op interview.

"What sort of operation are you having?" he asked.

"A crotch lift," said she. The doctor ducked his head, snickered, and covered his mouth.

"Do you have false teeth?" "No, do you?" The doctor giggled again.

"Do you wear a hearing aid?" "*What?*"

He was so charmed by this saucy patient that he dropped in to see her a couple of times after her operation.

Lucille's spontaneous witticisms enliven our art class; we all love her. Her husband has a matching sense of humor. She was planting rosebushes one afternoon when Harry came out to see what she was doing. "Would you like some help?" he asked. At that moment Lucille committed an inadvertent social error.

"A simple no would suffice," said Harry.

The publishing contract is such a long story, even I won't attempt to relate it. A simple "Yay" will suffice. Fran Allen and I still can't believe our efforts of three summers ago are going to produce a children's book based on Mother's verses. I'm hoping the right people will be so impressed with her work that they'll seek me out, looking for more. She was too great a poet to be forgotten.

Your letter deserves an A plus, though I think there was

one minor error. As I recall it, we were kissing in the hall, and my question was "What do you want to do?" Your answer, "I want to love you," had more class than my question.

Ed's marriage seems to be thriving. Aliceann goes fishing with him, cooks gourmet meals every night, and concerns herself with priorities like ring-around-the-collar. She was born to be a wife and homemaker. They have both been wonderful to me, so I haven't lost an ex-husband, I've gained a sister.

Thank you for your birthday message. Graceful Graduation. You do turn a nice phrase, Chris.

June 5, 1987
Weymouth

To Chris

I'm feeling fine, thank you, but I'm worried about you. When I read your latest casserole invention, I conjured up a vision of Chris turning into a pillar of salt. There was only one ingredient not loaded with sodium—the brown sugar.

Maybe I'm in no position to give pointers on keeping fit but I will, anyway. Are you including fresh fruit and vegetables in your diet? Less beef, more fish and chicken? I gave you my Freezer Lecture a couple of years ago, so I'll spare you a rehash. You can freeze hash, too.

To answer your question about the state of *my* health, I like to think the diagnosis was a silly mistake. I felt the same way when I amended my will six months ago. Two witnesses came in to sign the solemn document and I said, "This whole thing is ridiculous. I'm not going to die." Everybody laughed. The truth is, I know it could have been cancer and someday I'll die when I'm good and ready.

Family reunion, 1988. Front: *Lauren, Katie, Ed, Kathie, Sarah.* Rear: *Barbara, Ted, Maureen, Tim, Kathy, Janeth, Dick.*

August 15, 1987
Weymouth

To my cousin Florence

Dear Flo:

I have my typewriter (Mom's Smith-Corona, actually) back from the repair shop and feel better equipped to respond to your letter.

My Kathie is busy with her career as a psychology professor at Boston University and is the main support of her family while Dick works toward getting his master's degree and doctorate at B.U.

Ted is now in the construction business. He sold his swordfishing boat as he wanted to spend more time with his family. Young Teddy and Katie are thriving, as is their new baby brother, Gregory Michael. I wished I had my camera handy when Teddy opened a book and showed it to Greg, who, at two months, isn't quite ready for reading. Teddy and Katie are book lovers, and I am known at the maternal grandparents' beach house as the Book Lady. "Any books, Isha?" has been my greeting since the kids were toddlers. One of my favorite pictures shows me reading aloud, surrounded by my grandchildren and half a dozen neighborhood youngsters.

My younger son, Tim, married last fall about the time he turned forty. His wife, Kathy, is a sweetheart, and what's more, she came with a bonus—five-year-old Lauren. Lauren is a charming extrovert who continually amuses us with her precocious comments and insights. When she and her mother visited Maureen and the new baby in the hospital, Lauren wanted to know if Gregory still had his biblical cord. I'm hoping Tim, like Ted, will find some other line of work, as the fishing trips entail long separations, which Kathy finds hard to cope with.

I'm so glad you approve of our book [*Poetry with a Purpose*, a collection of my mother's poems designed to encourage children to read and write poetry]. I bless my co-editor daily for coming up with such a wonderful idea. She credits me with persistence in marketing our brainchild. Inside her typewriter case, Mom had taped a quotation, now faded and torn at the edges, "Persistence," by Calvin Coolidge: "Nothing in the world will take the place of persistence. Talent will not; there is nothing more common than unsuccessful men with talent. Genius will not; unrewarded genius is almost a proverb. Education will not. The world is full of educated derelicts. Persistence and determination alone are omnipotent. The slogan: 'Press on' has solved and always will solve the problems of the human race."

October 17, 1987
Weymouth

To Chris

I spent a couple of days at Migis Lodge in Maine with Tim, his bride, Kathy, and five-year-old Lauren. The latter kept us entertained with her Laurenisms. She tried one of the fried clams she'd ordered for lunch and announced, "These are the best fried clams I've had in years!" Tim officially adopted her this month. Lauren was disappointed at the hearing because, as she told the judge, she thought he'd say, "Do you, Lauren, take this man, Timmy, to be your lawful daddy?" Deciding the idea had merit, the judge led Lauren and Timmy through this variation on marriage vows.

I like the enclosed article [in the local paper] about *Poetry with a Purpose*, although I would have preferred the description "free-lance writer" to "lifelong writer." It's my own fault for answering the question "How long have you been interested in writing?" with "All my life." It sounds as if I were churning out a dozen novels a year. A dozen articles in twenty years is more like it.

Fran and I have received our first royalties on the 750 copies sold nationwide within three months after publication. It delights me to picture all these unknown teachers and parents looking at our book and deciding to buy it. Grace Lawrence's illustrations mirror Mother's whimsical humor, adding sparkle to every page.

November 7, 1987
Weymouth

To Aliceann

I'm glad to hear Ed's problem is so much better. On the phone last night, Chris asked how he was doing since his operation. I said, "I think he's stopped leaking."

There was a shocked silence. "Oh, I *hope* not," Chris said. Then he told me about the terrible time he'd had in the hospital when he had *his* prostate operation. He'd reached a point where he couldn't have leaked if he wanted to, and he wanted to. Feeling ready to burst any minute, he asked the nurse to get the doctor in a hurry.

"There was a male nurse I'd noticed when I first came in. He was gay, no question about it, and I said to myself, 'I'm never gonna let *that* guy anywhere near me, no sir!'"

Fast forward to Chris's hospital room, where he is ready to die of blockage of the bladder. "When this gay chap walked in with the catheter, my feelings about him changed immediately. He was gonna take away the pain. I wanted to say, 'Do with me what you will. Take me, I'm yours. *Dahrling!*'"

Did Ed tell you about our little skirmish at Kathie and Dick's? I had driven him there so Dick could take him to the airport early in the morning. He unloaded his stuff from my car, leaving one suitcase to the left of the driveway while everything else was lined up on the right. "You'd better put this over with that," I said. He sighed and grumbled and wanted to know why. "Well, things *can* get forgotten or mislaid—remember how you walked off with Dick's keys?" He grumbled some more. "I'm just being rational," I said—to which he replied, "I call it n-a-g-g-i-n-g. Why do you women always have to have things *your* way?"

Edward, you're funny and we love you, don't we, Aliceann. You just need feminine guidance now and then.

July 28, 1988
Weymouth

Ed has been at Mass. General Hospital for three weeks, a nervous wreck while he waits for triple-bypass surgery to be scheduled. By his own admission, he doesn't have the resources for such a trial. I offered to help him pass the time by teaching him to run this computer, but he wasn't interested. He wants only for the damn doctors to get their act together so he can go back to Florida. A nurse said to him, "When is it you expect to have surgery, Mr. Malley?" He gave her a wry look and said, " . . . When you're a grandmother."

Aliceann came north a week ago when we thought he was finally going to have the operation. Then the surgeon decided he didn't like the look of his carotid-arteries report and called off the heart surgery. Two days of conferences were followed by the decree that Ed will have back-to-back operations for both problems tomorrow.

Is there a God who hears our prayers? Long ago I came to a conclusion that satisfies me: who knows? I'm putting my faith in the doctors at Mass. General and in Ed's stubbornness.

July 29, 1988
Weymouth

Ed called at 9:30 last night to tell me he loved me and to "say good-bye" (no, no, Ed, fare-*well*), and to thank me for all the happy years we had together. I told him I'd just finished writing about our courtship and was more than ever aware of how much I loved him and how difficult I'd been (*Never*, he said). He asked me to pray for him. I am.

July 31, 1988
Weymouth

Yesterday Aliceann and I held hands during Ed's operation. We held each of his after it was over. Last night, after leaving Mass. General Hospital, we had dinner at the golf club. We cheered each other with reminiscences about our favorite husband.

A couple stopped at our table as they were leaving the dining room. Before I had a chance to introduce them, Jeanette said, "Frank and I have a bet. We've been watching you two, and we're sure you must be sisters."

Aliceann and I beamed at each other. "We are," I said. "We're the two Mrs. Malleys."

September 17, 1988
Weymouth
To Chris

Kathie has had some good news. Boston University's President John Silber notified her that she was to receive the "University Scholar/Teacher of the Year Award." Along with the award is an honorarium of two thousand dollars. I talked to her last night after she and Dick attended the reception at President Silber's house. She was happy about Silber's praise when he announced the award and about the many congratulations she received from her colleagues. The United Methodist Church initiated this award four years ago, and it has been won by two women and two men. One of the women is Lynne Margoulis, a nationally known biologist who has received other prestigious honors. Kathie sounded a bit overwhelmed at being in such fancy company. As unassuming as ever, she encourages her students to call her by her first name. *I* like to call her "Dr. White, my daughter the psychologist." Do I sound like a proud mama? I am! Kathie's friends are urging her not to use the two thousand for bills but to go to Ireland with Dick, a trip they've been talking about for years. She's convinced they're right and plans to go next spring. That's all the news for now, Chris dear.

December 7, 1988
Weymouth

To Chris

Something funny happened today. I woke up with a fit of sneezing and nose blowing that went on all day. I knew it wasn't a cold but an allergy. To the holiday season, maybe. I could hardly function at Kathie's, I was so busy attending to the dripping faucet my nose had become. Finally I resorted to a stopgap I have used when alone in my condominium. I stuffed a Kleenex tissue in my nose and just let it hang there; the improvised filter didn't improve my appearance, but it cut down on the sneezing.

I was sitting in the dining room, concentrating on Kathie's files, when I heard eight-year-old Sarah call my name. "Yes, Sarah?" I said, continuing my work. After a long silence I looked up to see what she wanted. She was standing in the doorway, staring at me. I laughed so hard the Kleenex fell off my face. When I told Kathie and Dick what had happened, he said, "She probably thought you were Santa Claus."

Regarding Ed's remarriage, my only negative feeling is a tinge of regret that he wasn't content to go along as we had for twelve years, with partially shared lives and interests. But he didn't like being single, and I'm sure he's happier now. My friends and family keep me from being lonely, and of course I look forward to your letters. Whoever said of east and west that never the twain shall meet didn't have a Chris to correspond with. I mustn't end with a preposition, so I'll say
Love and Happy New Year

December 9, 1988
Weymouth

To Ed Brecher

It's been exactly fifty years today since I first met Ed Malley, nearly forty-nine years since I married him, fourteen years since I divorced him, and just short of three years since he married the woman of my choice, the maker of the world's best apple strudel.

Here's the story, the way it felt to me while it was happening. Rereading it all now, I'm amazed at how little I'd want to change.

Ed is now seventy-three, I'm sixty-seven, and our lives go on as always. Indeed, Ed phoned this afternoon.

"Happy anniversary," I said.

"That's not what I called about."

"What did you call about?"

"I just wanted you to know that, if I weren't so happily married to Aliceann, I'd marry you and *double* your alimony."

In Loving Memory

For those who enriched and inspired my life:

Children's poet, Ernestine Cobern Beyer, my mother and dream nourisher (1893–1972)

Beloved Beyer family nurse and lifetime caregiver, Vaughan Ross (1875–1962)

Blithe spirit, Stephanie Vaughan Malley (Vonnie), my sorely missed daughter (1945–1976)

Wisest of mentors, fellow traveler, Floyd Rinker (1901–1988)

Favorite correspondent and motivator, Darrell McClure (1904–1987)

And, finally, I gratefully acknowledge my debt to valued friend and adviser Edward M. Brecher. With his selfless and unconditional help, I started this book in 1988. I only regret that he didn't live to see it completed and welcomed by Roger Donald, his former editor at Little, Brown and Company.